Diagrams
Innovative Solutions for Graphic Designers

Carolyn Knight and Jessica Glaser

RotoVision

A RotoVision Book

Published and distributed by RotoVision SA
Route Suisse 9
CH-1295 Mies
Switzerland

RotoVision SA
Sales and Editorial Office
Sheridan House, 114 Western Road
Hove BN3 1DD, UK

Tel: +44 (0)1273 72 72 68
Fax: +44 (0)1273 72 72 69
www.rotovision.com

10 9 8 7 6 5 4 3 2

ISBN: 978-2-88893-061-7

Art Direction: Tony Seddon
Design: Lisa Båtsvik-Miller
Cover design: Lisa Båtsvik-Miller
Icons on disc: Emily Portnoi and Anette Mosdøl
Set in Unit and Kontrapunkt

Reprographics in Singapore by ProVision Pte.
Tel: +65 6334 7720
Fax: +65 6334 7721

Printed in China by 1010 Printing International Ltd.

Contents

Introduction

In today's increasingly visually oriented and global world, designers are required to present more and more information in visual form. This data has to be swiftly and successfully communicated to a wide range of audiences, both nationally and internationally. This creates a multiplicity of challenges for any designer. *Diagrams* showcases a varied selection of the best contemporary information graphics from around the world; it discusses communication methods and looks at designers' inspirations. It provides an excellent visual source of ideas for all types of tabular and diagrammatic information, as well as including a CD of ready-to-use, copyright-free symbols that designers can adapt and personalize for use in their own work.

There are no rules or regulations as to what has to be included in a visual interpretation of data, so long as it communicates in a manner that can be understood. As Edward Tufte suggested, "To envision information is to work at the intersection of image, word, number, art." (*Envisioning Information*, Edward R. Tufte). Any images, marks, and text can be used. *Diagrams* introduces readers to an exceptional standard and variety of imaginative information graphics that incorporate a whole raft of techniques.

Human interaction relies on our insatiable desire to make sense of what is being communicated. This is not to say that designers can pull anything together in the sure knowledge that readers will be able to decipher the result. However, it does mean that they can generally rely on readers *wanting* to understand the information

being presented to them. People have an automatic tendency to group elements, discern hierarchies, and tease out the sequencing of information, and the examples in this book demonstrate that diagrams, providing the designs are skillfully handled, are not only more easily understood, but are also more interesting and enjoyable to read than text alone. Simplicity is not necessarily the key to successful communication; several layers of information can make for an exciting visual experience as a whole, and these layers can be broken down clearly into different levels through changes in color and styles of mark-making, through contrasts in scale, and through spatial distribution.

Color is particularly useful in the design of diagrams, maps, and tables because not only can readers differentiate between a vast number of hues, they can also recognize many variations in tone and saturation. Contrasting muted colors with vibrant spot colors can make for aesthetically pleasing designs that knock back less important information and bring out key points. As Paul Klee says, "And what tremendous possibilities for the variation of meaning are offered by the combination of colors... What variations from the smallest shading to the glowing symphony of color. What perspectives in the dimension of meaning!" Of course, it is essential for designers to make visual judgments when selecting colors for information graphics, as the perception of color is always relative. Any one color can appear entirely different when placed on different-colored backgrounds and, as a result, can upset any efficiency of carefully chosen color coding.

Most diagrams involve making connections of some kind; designers are required to create a type of visual shorthand that relates or links elements clearly, but they rarely have the luxury of being true to scale or spatial implications, and often have to work without the use of verbal language. Maps in particular are frequently too complicated to show a great deal of geography, but they do need to demonstrate how places are connected, and they must also communicate some aspect of spatial information. *Diagrams* showcases many examples of interesting solutions for connecting devices, from graphs, tables, and the use of icons such as arrows, to more sophisticated and often more stimulating concepts.

Diagrammatic data informs on both a macro and a micro level. Initially the reader gets a general impression of what is being communicated, then on closer inspection engages in more detailed matters. A simple demonstration of this could be any design that includes lists of names. The macro level perhaps indicates vast quantities of people, or in the case of a family tree, that there are many members on one side of the family and few on the other; the micro level gives the names and sex of these people. A number of examples in this book use the macro level to create a visually exciting and enticing first level, with the intention of persuading readers to take time to understand the micro information.

Essentially, the visualization of information involves summarizing and honing given data so that it can be presented in a succinct manner. Designers frequently have to make difficult decisions about what information to include and what to omit. Highly sophisticated software enables amendments to be made comparatively swiftly and easily right up until the last minute. In Robert Spence's words, "A graphic is no longer 'drawn' once and for all: it is constructed and reconstructed (manipulated) until all the relationships which lie within it have been perceived … a graphic is never an end in itself: it is a moment in the process of decision making." (*Information Visualisation*.)

Far from being a catalog of functional and technical designs, *Diagrams*' pages are overflowing with exciting, innovative material. Many of the examples could only function as diagrams, but a number of designers chose to utilize a diagrammatic design when another form of design would also have worked. If information graphics were once considered uninspiring and lacking in creativity, the contemporary design solutions in this book provide a totally different and fascinating perspective.

Pamela Zuccker Allyson Lack

Ricky Tillblad Florian Sebald

Tom Muller Nelleke Wegdam

Russell Hancock MAKI

1.

310k Richard Sarson Jonas Banker C
MAKI Todd Houlette Robbie Graha
Lucy Hibburd Sion Phillips F
Billy Kiosoglou Franck Gentil
Ida Wessel Jerry Hsiao Nelleke

Branding & Promotion

Chris Bolton Kee-Ling Turner
Todd Houlette Robbie Graham MAKI Sion Phillips
Russell Hancock Lucy Hibburd Jerry Hsiao
Richard Sarson Jones Banke
Dirkje Bakker Tom Mulle
310K

on Jason Mu
ell Hancock
ilipp
nn

CITIES OF THE WORLD
Design by Richard Sarson

Client: AECOM/Faber Maunsell for
OPX Communications Design
Design firm: Richard Sarson Art & Design

This design installation was based
on the worldwide sites of the eight
headquarters of AECOM and their
relationships to the locations of
the company's other 280 regional
offices. The installation demonstrates
how facts and figures can be used to
create fascinating, abstract patterns.

reference

Designer Richard Sarson took his
inspiration from "the simplicity and
beauty of data." The resulting diagrams
are reminiscent of airline flight maps.

NORDIC PACK
Design by Jerry Hsiao

Client: Nike
Design firm: Staple Design
Art direction: Jeff Ng

This design uses the diagrammatic properties of maps combined with other intriguing elements to create a visual narrative. The maps themselves, although recognizable as specific locations, could not be used as a route finder, or to pinpoint geographic detail.

Each design tells an imaginary story about travel to one of three renowned Winter Olympics: Lillehammer in 1994, Nagano in 1998, and Salt Lake City in 2002. The location of these designs adds detail to the stories. The map, passport stamps, and luggage labels are printed on the insoles of Nike footwear, implying that the owners of these Nike shoes are ardent winter sport fans, with a history of attending, or participating in, Winter Olympics events.

Jeff Ng says, "The ideas behind this design came from old luggage tags, passport stamps, and maps. We wanted to relay the feeling of having traveled to the Winter Olympics, and also to imply a more personal story for the owner of the shoe."

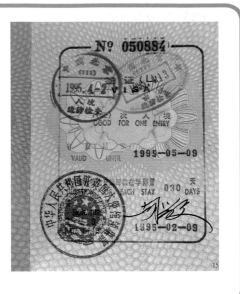

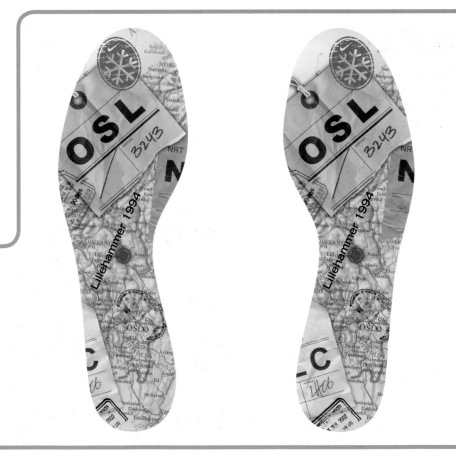

HUDSONS COFFEE STORE LOCATORS
Design by MAKI

Client: Hail Design
Design firm: MAKI
Art direction: Jason Stancombe
　　at Hail Design

Hudsons Coffee stores are renowned for quality coffee. MAKI wanted to reflect the bespoke service they offer in the design of their location maps, and used an individual style of execution to reflect the distinctive quality of the Hudsons product. Roads are indicated with hand-drawn lines that are reversed white through an orange background; all typographic details appear hand-rendered and are shown white through red or green boxes; and a number of cute icons are used to represent and pinpoint popular locations such as a market, information center, or beach.

The orange background, reminiscent of the typical takeout brown-paper bag, has been subtly augmented with coffee-cup rings and handwritten "invitations" to come in for coffee.

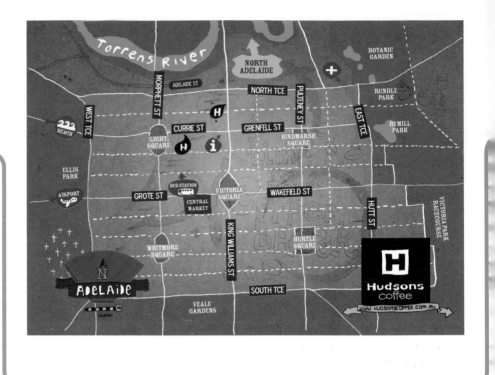

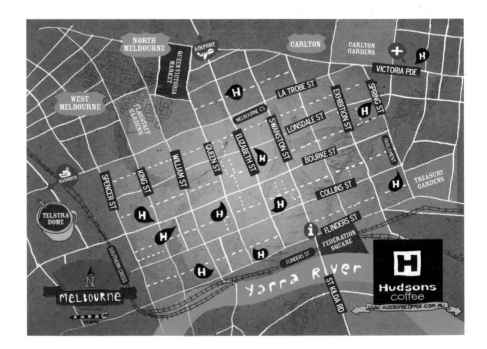

MASON: BIGBOY COVER
Design by 310k

Client: Middle of the Road Records
Design firm: 310k
Art direction: 310k

A diagrammatic interpretation is not the most obvious approach to the design for a record sleeve, but that is the route 310k took for this Mason release. This sleeve design features a mix of "found" technical drawings that are connected through a range of cables, wires, and plugs. Line drawings of such diverse items as cogs, wheels, early electronic keyboards, ventilation shafts, satellites, and a weight-lifter's bench have been brought together as a way of representing the skills and knowledge, as well as the technology, that are necessary in the creation of a piece of electronic music. The reader is left to imagine the sound of electronic music being gradually built up, layer by layer, as it progresses from item to item to its ultimate destination—the cassette player on the back of the album sleeve.

reference

The technical drawings, which became a main feature of this design, were the visual inspiration for this piece.

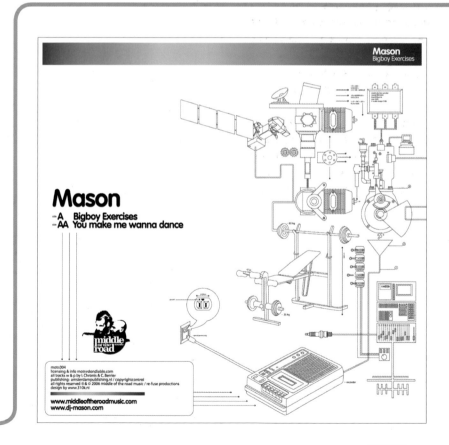

CUSTOMIZED PANELS FOR HFT STUDIO, CHICAGO
Design by Jonas Banker

Client: John Hughes at HFT Studio, Chicago
Design firm: BankerWessel
Art direction: Jonas Banker and John Hughes
Illustration: Jonas Banker

High-specification music-studio equipment often features specialized information design to help technicians and producers find their way around the complex banks of electronic modules. BankerWessel have taken this idea one step further to produce diagrammatic panels that show plugs arranged in groups that can be joined up with colorful linework to form figurative images. Surfing stick figures, sharks, ducks, turkeys, and cars are some of the images created.

reference

Jonas Banker comments, "The inspiration for these designs came from the work of Japanese artist Takeo Takei." Takei was born in 1894 and studied at the Western-style art department of Tokyo Art School in 1919. After graduation he made his name specializing in illustration for children, founding the Japan Association of Illustration for Children in 1927.

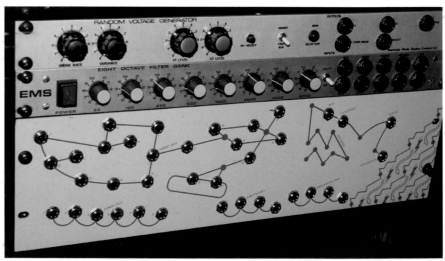

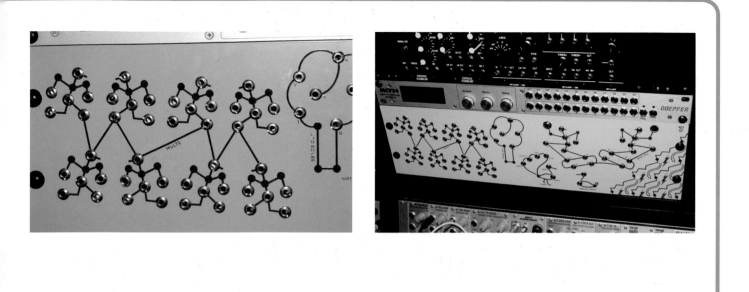

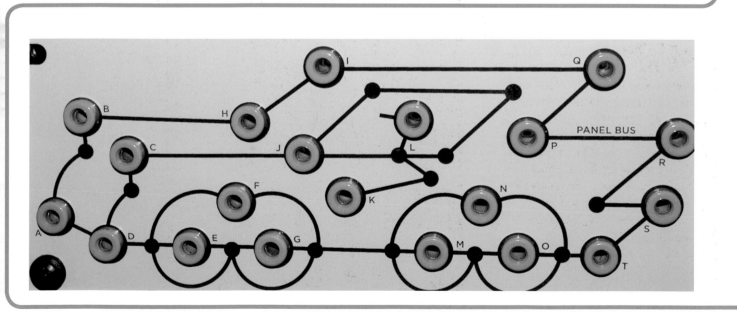

**REVERSO 68: TOKYO DISCO
AND ESPECIAL**
Design by Chris Bolton

Client: Eskimo Recordings (parent
label, N.E.W.S.)
Design firm: Chris Bolton
Art direction: Chris Bolton
Typography: Chris Bolton

These album covers are interesting
examples of diagrammatic design being
used even though the context does not
demand this kind of solution. Designer
Chris Bolton decided to form each letter
of the album title using dashed arrows.
The arrows were positioned to reinforce
the directional element within each
letterform, emphasizing curves, angles,
and corners, as well as the extreme
thickness of each individual letterform.

Bolton's inspiration for this came
quite by chance; while looking for
a typographic design for the project,
he began to experiment with options
for creating dashed and dotted rules,
complete with arrowheads and tails,
and followed that through in the
design of the entire piece.

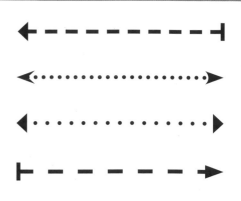

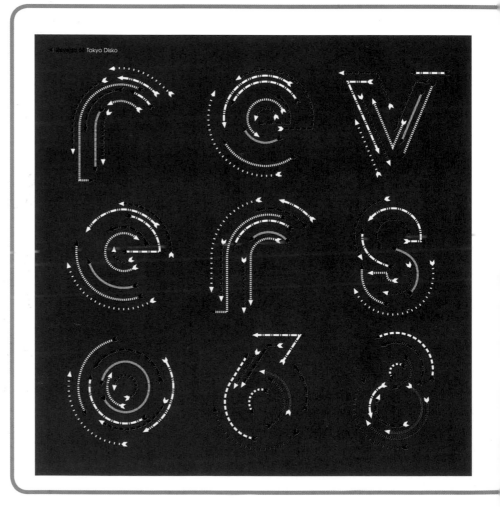

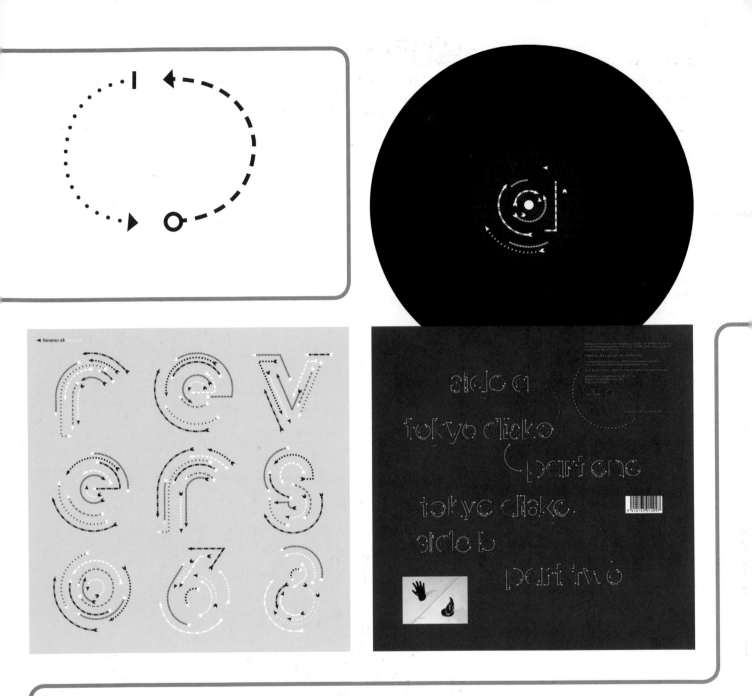

BIJ JANSEN TABLECLOTH AND PLACE MAT
Design by MAKI

Client: Bij Jansen
Design firm: MAKI
Art direction: MAKI
Illustration: MAKI

This submission proves that diagrams really do find a role in every walk of life. MAKI's diagrammatic design for café restaurant Bij Jansen was for a tablecloth and place mat. These pieces feature a mix of naive hand-drawn illustrations of plates, cutlery, fish, and vegetables, and cutout photos of farm animals. The place mat not only indicates how to set the table, showing where to place the knife and fork, it also informs diners where each cut of meat comes from, and passes visual comment on the conditions necessary for rearing quality meat.

The tablecloth acts as one large diagram. As well as protecting the table from food and drink spills, it identifies the seating

positions for eight diners. The cloth can also be used as a board game or coloring mat for children. Each place setting is slightly different, featuring individual illustration and annotation.

reference

MAKI cite the historic Dutch board game Ganzenbord, otherwise known as "the game of the goose," as their inspiration for this work. The game, which features a goose progressing around a track of consecutively numbered spaces, has been played for centuries. When a player throws a number that lands them on a space with the image of a goose, he or she is able to move forward by the same number of spaces again.

NIKE FOOTWEAR TECHNOLOGY PACKAGE
Design by Todd Houlette

Client: Nike Asia Pacific
Design firm: Plazm
Art direction: Joshua Berger

Plazm was commissioned to produce point-of-purchase designs for Nike to advertise the primary benefits of four models of Nike footwear. Its solution was to use charts to plot the cushioning, stability, and responsiveness of each shoe using rows of filled-in circles; the greater the number of orange dots, the greater the benefit provided.

reference

The inspiration for these designs was the technical detail of Nike footwear design. A range of Nike technical drawings is used to demonstrate how impact and weight affect the complex structure and cushioning within the sports shoe. These detailed diagrams provide a rare glimpse of the internal design of the product.

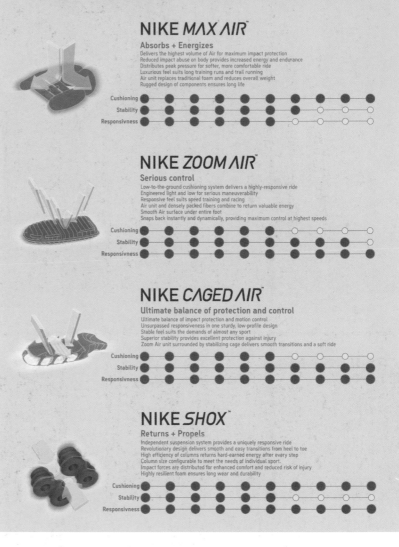

FIND THE SHOE DESIGNED TO MEET YOUR ATHLETIC NEEDS

NIKE MAX AIR
Absorbs + Energizes
Delivers the highest volume of Air for maximum impact protection
Reduced impact abuse on body provides increased energy and endurance
Distributes peak pressure for softer, more comfortable ride
Luxurious feel suits long training runs and trail running
Air unit replaces traditional foam and reduces overall weight
Rugged design of components ensures long life

Cushioning
Stability
Responsivness

NIKE ZOOM AIR
Serious control
Low-to-the-ground cushioning system delivers a highly-responsive ride
Engineered light and low for serious maneuverability
Responsive feel suits speed training and racing
Air unit and densely packed fibers combine to return valuable energy
Smooth Air surface under entire foot
Snaps back instantly and dynamically, providing maximum control at highest speeds

Cushioning
Stability
Responsivness

NIKE CAGED AIR
Ultimate balance of protection and control
Ultimate balance of impact protection and motion control
Unsurpassed responsiveness in one sturdy, low-profile design
Stable feel suits the demands of almost any sport
Superior stability provides excellent protection against injury
Zoom Air unit surrounded by stabilizing cage delivers smooth transitions and a soft ride

Cushioning
Stability
Responsivness

NIKE SHOX
Returns + Propels
Independent suspension system provides a uniquely responsive ride
Revolutionary design delivers smooth and easy transitions from heel to toe
High efficiency of columns returns hard-earned energy after every step
Column size configurable to meet the needs of individual sport
Impact forces are distributed for enhanced comfort and reduced risk of injury
Highly resilient foam ensures long wear and durability

Cushioning
Stability
Responsivness

NIKE SHOX

Returns + propels
Independent suspension system provides a uniquely responsive ride
Revolutionary design delivers smooth and easy transitions from heel to toe

NIKE CAGED AIR

Ultimate balance of protection and control
Ultimate balance of impact protection and motion control
Unsurpassed responsiveness in one sturdy, low-profile design

NIKE MAX AIR

Absorbs + energizes
Delivers the highest volume of Air for maximum impact protection
Reduced impact abuse on body provides increased energy and endurance

NIKE ZOOM AIR

Serious control
Low-to-the-ground cushioning system delivers a highly-responsive ride
Engineered light and low for serious maneuverability

GADGETSHOP
**Design by Robbie Graham,
Russell Hancock, Lucy Hibburd,
and Sion Phillips**

Client: The Entertainer
Design firm:
  ArthurSteenHorneAdamson
Creative direction: Marksteen
  Adamson and Scott McGuffie
Typography: Marksteen Adamson
  and Scott McGuffie
Illustration: Robbie Graham and
  Russell Hancock
Photography: John Hytch

Gadgetshop markets a range of quirky products. Items such as USB cup warmers, coin sorters, water rockets, and chocolate fountains have been distinctively packaged and promoted by ArthurSteenHorneAdamson. All of the Gadgetshop packaging, promotional posters, and stationery features memorable line diagrams.

reference

The simple information graphics and line drawings take their style from scientific diagrams; special features are clearly highlighted with annotations, while instructions for using the products are given in the form of clear, sequential illustrations. The designers comment that the character Q from the James Bond movies was their inspiration. "We like the way every Bond movie takes gadgets so seriously, and the way Q delivers his new inventions to Bond."

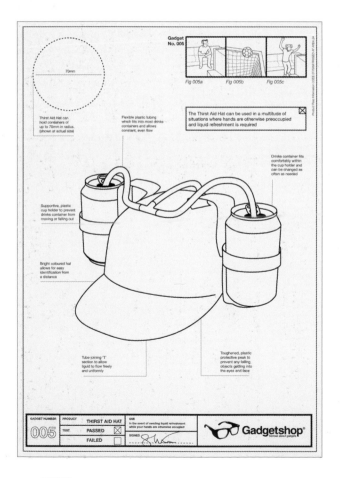

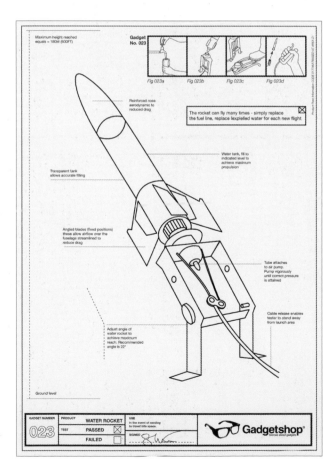

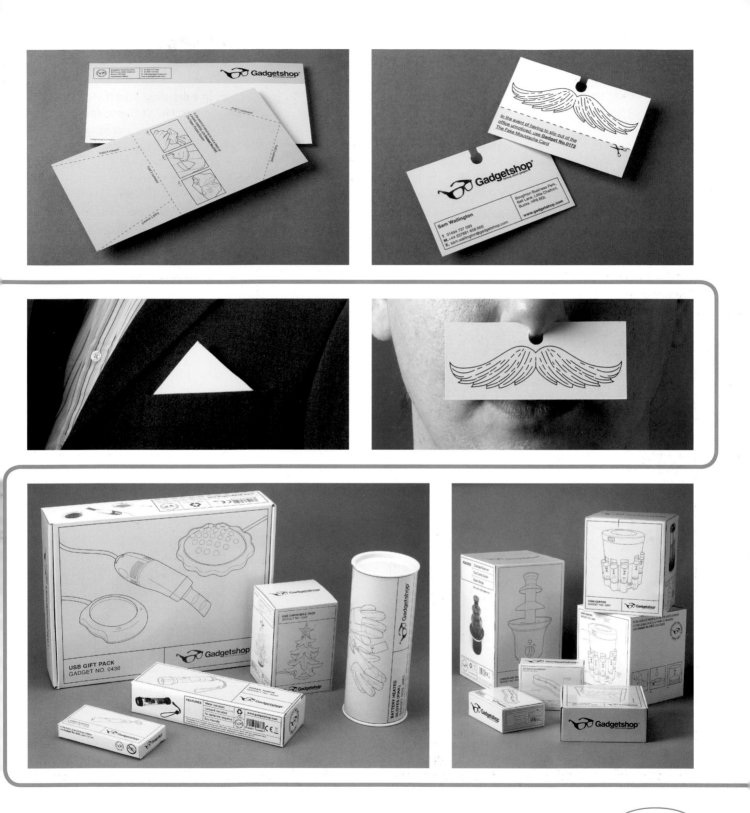

DASMANGO: SPOIL YOUR SUMMER
Design by Frank Philippin and Billy Kiosoglou

Client: Grundlos Records
Design firm: Brighten the Corners
Art direction: Frank Philippin and
 Billy Kiosoglou
Photography: Frank Philippin

The cover of Dasmango's *Spoil Your Summer* makes use of sequential images to tell a story. The images are arranged in linear order, taking the viewer on a bus journey from the depot, along a lengthy highway, to the coast and the final destination of a sparsely populated, rather gray beach.

reference

The method of storytelling was inspired by postcards—not just any cards, but the older, less popular designs that remain in the store rack and fade. "Within the design for this CD, we have represented the age of the card by using the color spectrum, and not featuring magenta, as this is the first color to fade in sunlight," says Philippin. Throughout the design, Philippin and Kiosoglou have used image boxes with curved corners to reinforce the idea of these postcards.

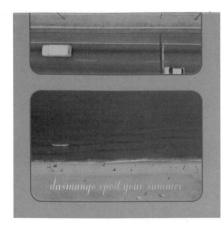

LIPTON KOMBUCHA
**Design by Franck Gentil
and Kee-Ling Turner**

Client: Unilever
Design firm: Beam
Art direction: Franck Gentil
Typography: Kee-Ling Turner
Illustration: Kee-Ling Turner
Photography: Adrian Lander

"The idea behind this map for Kombucha was to provide publicity for this 'ancient drink for a new world,'" says designer Franck Gentil. Each country is represented by a distinctive pattern. For example, the dot patterns, which for many have become symbolic of Aboriginal artwork, are used to denote Australia; and the jagged designs of Native American textiles are used to represent the USA. Using these familiar and culturally significant designs removes the need for typographic detail, which means that product publicity and packaging can communicate effectively to many cultures without any translation.

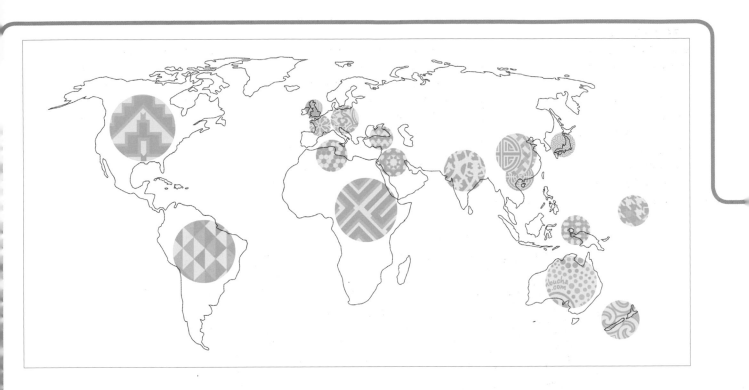

reference

The map and the packaging take their inspiration from the traditional patterns and designs of different cultures, as well as the bright-yellow tones symbolic of the brand.

MAP OF THE WORLD
Design by Ida Wessel

Client: Swedish Institute
Design firm: BankerWessel
Art direction: Ida Wessel
Illustration: Jonas Banker

This map of the world was produced to illustrate the fact that the Swedish Institute is involved with cultural events around the world. Although this design does not allow the reader to pinpoint locations with any accuracy, the extensive use of bright color and dynamic visual rhythm conveys a sense of vivacity, excitement, and a zest for life.

reference

BankerWessel was hugely influenced by the work of Italian architect and designer Ettore Sottsass, who was a founding member of the 1980s design movement Memphis. Sottsass referred to Memphis as "the new international style," as it offered a bright and lively contrast to the darker colors evident in European furniture design.

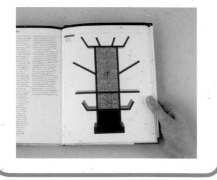

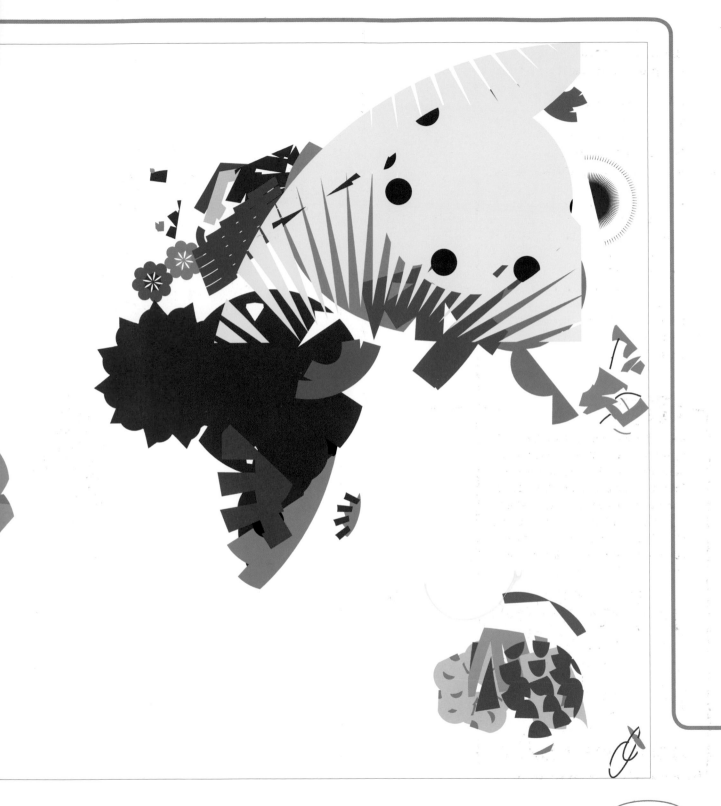

**STEVE ANGELLO AND LAIDBACK
LUKE: OTHERWIZE THEN**
Design by Ricky Tillblad

Client: Refune
Design firm: Zion Graphics
Art direction: Ricky Tillblad
Typography: Ricky Tillblad
Illustration: Ricky Tillblad

reference

The inspiration for this design came from lunar maps and UK children's television series *Teletubbies*, which features four brightly colored characters who live in a landscape of rolling, grassy hills.

Ricky Tillblad of Zion Graphics was commissioned to design this CD cover for Otherwize Then. His solution features a contour map printed and varnished on the back cover. The peaks and troughs are used to locate markers that contain the CD's credits and production information.

MODEST MOUSE CONCERT POSTER
Design by Jason Munn

Client: Modest Mouse
Design firm: The Small Stakes
Illustration: Jason Munn

The inspiration behind this creation was "the off-kilter lyrics of Modest Mouse," says Munn.

Many diagrams are visualizations of a change, or of a process taking place. In this concert poster Jason Munn shows the bizarre evolution from old-fashioned telephone dial to well-camouflaged snake. Within his design, Munn has used the circumference of the traditional telephone dial for the girth of the snake's body, and the circular finger holes of the dial for its distinctive patterning.

BPC Camping Tour
Design by Florian Sebald

Client: Bpitchcontrol.de
Design firm: Pfadfinderei

reference

"The theme and inspiration was camping," says Sebald of Pfadfinderei, "with guy lines pulled taut to secure a fly sheet stretched into the shape of Europe."

This distinctive map was designed to show the viewer the many countries visited by musicians on the Bpitchcontrol label on their various tours. In this illustration, Europe is represented as though guy ropes have been attached to the edges of the continent. The visualized stretching of fabric gives rounded bays and curved edges to peninsulas. Although the outlines of the landmasses are hugely simplified, it is still easy to recognize the distinctive shapes of Europe.

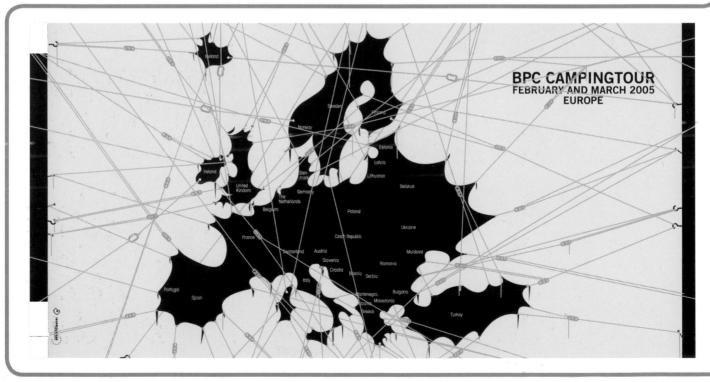

NAPASTYLE TISSUE PAPER
**Design by Pamela Zuccker
and Allyson Lack**

Client: NapaStyle
Design firm: Principle
Art direction: Pamela Zuccker
Typography: James Noel Smith
Illustration: James Noel Smith

Chef Michael Chiarello believes in using distinctive salts, sourced from around the world. This tissue paper, used for packaging in the NapaStyle store, was designed to communicate this. It features specially commissioned pen-and-ink maps which detail the salt-producing regions of Peru, Sicily, Brittany, Hawaii, and Utah,

along with intriguing stories concerning the origins of sea salt. The individual sheets have qualities reminiscent of treasure maps.

Pamela Zuccker comments, "As so many people relate to Michael on a personal level because of his Emmy Award–winning show, it was necessary to give his voice a strong presence throughout the design. Michael cooks with salt from all over the world. He is interested in how minerals in the water or the conditions under which it forms determine a salt's flavor."

reference

Michael's mantra is, "If you change one thing about your cooking, make it the salt." In Zuccker's words, "we used this quote as an inspiration to share a piece of Michael's story with every customer purchase."

HARDTROZE FLYER
**Design by Dirkje Bakker
and Nelleke Wegdam**

Client: Hardtroze
Design firm: No Office
Art direction: Dirkje Bakker
  and Nelleke Wegdam
Typography: Dirkje Bakker
  and Nelleke Wegdam
Illustration: Dirkje Bakker
  and Nelleke Wegdam

reference

This design features a variety of diagrams inspired by the shapes of dingbats and asterisks found in a computer's font library.

Hardtroze is a popular Dutch bag label. For this promotional flyer, No Office used fictional statistical information to illustrate the life-lengthening results of purchasing a Hardtroze bag.

A pie chart purports to show the percentage of Hardtroze bags sold within the Netherlands, Europe, and the rest of the world. This pie chart is formed by the division of a carefully selected flower-shaped asterisk into three tonally different sections. The flower shape reinforces the amount of happiness purchases of Hardtroze bags have led to in these three areas of the world.

A simple bar chart with a complex key plots the reasons why men buy women Hardtroze bags, and the relationship between giver and receiver. Again, No Office used dingbats and symbols as indicators. For example, a heart is used to show a birthday purchase, a flower denotes a forgotten birthday, and a star symbolizes a purchase to show love. Each of these symbols sits within a square; four types of square are used to indicate four different relationships: girlfriend, prospective girlfriend, female relation, or female friend.

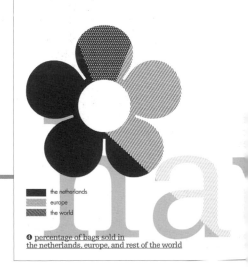

Hardtroze is a new and fresh brand of bags.
March 2003, 4 friends joined forces and put
their ideas together.
This resulted in their first collection of bags to
be admired on www.hardtroze.nl, launched at
18 october 2003.
The bags are hand made and every single one is
unique. Although every bag has its own design,
they have one thing in common: a deep pink
stitching or details. What makes hardtroze so
special is that it r
could never be bo
making it. Never u
evolves from a sin
never be mass pro

In conclusion: ha
fashion design.

❷ types of bags sold to women
and men according to age

>40
30-40
20-30
10-20
<10

www.hardtroze.nl

❶☞❹ get your bag now
or someone else will

❼ if your name starts
with a m or a s, chances
are you already own one

❻ hardtroze is 4 girls
and a whole heap
of bags

❷ research shows:
men like them too!

❸ customer survey
suggests: these bags
are too hot to handle

❺ making up for bad
behaviour has never
been this easy

❶❷❸❹❺❻❼ truths about hardtroze after extended customer research

graphic design / no office

girlfriend ♥ for their birthday
prospective girlfriend ✿ to show how much they love them
mother, sister, grandma ✿ forgot their birthday
female friend ✳ making up for bad behaviour

❹ reasons for men to buy women a hardtroze
bag and the relationship they have with them

❻ company growth

o ✳
p ✿❀✳✳
q
r ✦✳✳✳
s ✳✳✿✳✳✳✳✳ ●
t ✿✳ ✦
u ✳✳
v ✳
w
x ✳
y ✳
z ●✳

❼ number of bags sold to people according
to the first letter of their names

**PRINS THOMAS: COSMO
GALACTIC PRISM
Design by Chris Bolton**

Client: Eskimo Recordings/N.E.W.S
Art direction: Chris Bolton
Typography: Chris Bolton
Illustration: Chris Bolton

Eskimo Recordings asked Chris Bolton
to design the label and packaging for
Cosmo Galactic Prism, a compilation
album by DJ Prins Thomas. Rather than
set album details in standard print,
Bolton laid out the track listings and
other information in a diagrammatic
form, picking up on the title of the
album itself.

reference

The idea behind the typographic
arrangement comes from the title,
and specifically the word "prism."
In response to this, Bolton created
a prismatic "mark." This then inspired
him to create "prismatic" tables in
which to lay out the track listings of
the album—all type is set on a baseline
rotated to 45°. The cover illustration
was inspired by images from NASA
and the Hubble Space Telescope.

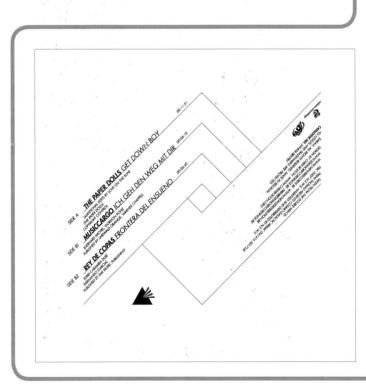

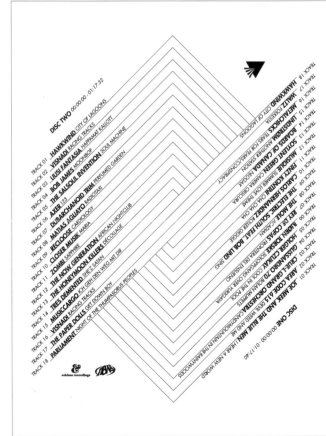

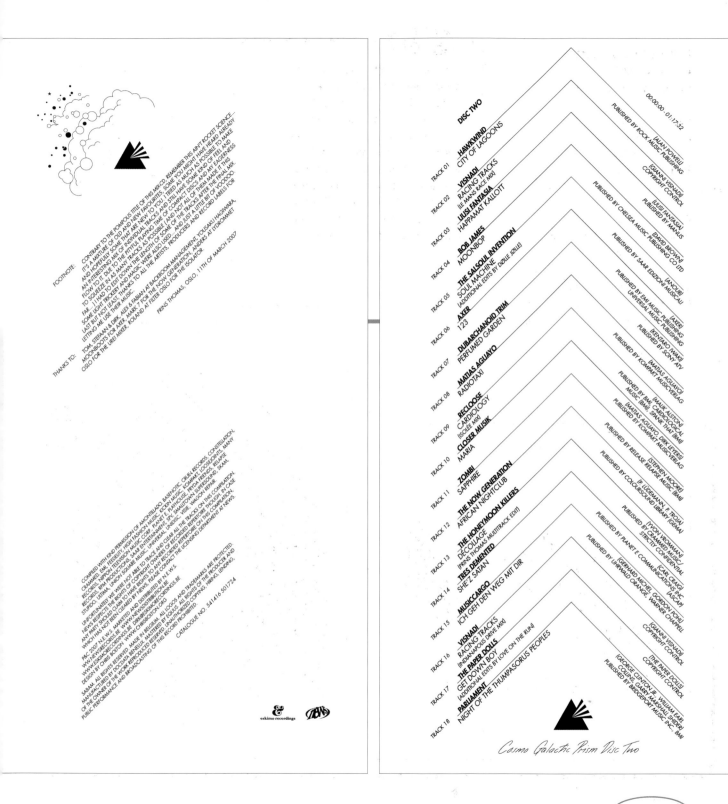

FOOTNOTE: CONTRARY TO THE POMPOUS TITLE OF THIS MIX-CD, REMEMBER THIS AIN'T ROCKET SCIENCE... IT'S A MIXTURE OF OLD AND NEW FAVOURITES. SOME YOU MIGHT HAVE HEARD ALREADY AND HOPEFULLY SOME THAT ARE NEW TO YOU. I TRIED AS MUCH AS POSSIBLE TO MAKE AN INTERESTING MIX OF INDIVIDUAL TRACKS AND STILL HAVE SOME KIND OF FEEL AND FLOW. IT DUE TO THE PITIFUL PLAYING TIME OF COMPACT DISCS AND MY EAGERNESS TO SQUEEZE IN AS MANY TRACKS AS POSSIBLE I DID NOT ALL OF THEM MADE IT THIS FAR...I HAD TO EDIT DOWN THE LENGTH OF SOME OF THE TRACKS AFTER THE FINAL MIX. SOME LIGHT TRICKERY AND MAGIC WERE ALSO USED...AND JUST A LITTLE BIT OF VOODOO. LAST BUT NOT LEAST, THANKS TO ALL THE ARTISTS, PRODUCERS AND RECORD LABELS FOR LETTING ME USE THEIR MUSIC.

PRINS THOMAS, OSLO, 11TH OF MARCH 2007

THANKS TO: TOM, STEFAAN & DIRK, ALEX & FABIAN AT BACKROOM MANAGEMENT, YOUSAKU HAGIWARA, MOONBOOTS FOR AXER, MARK 7, FOR THE NOW GENERATION, ANDERS AT LYDROMMET, OSLO FOR THE UREI MIXER, ROLAND AT FILTER OSLO FOR THE ISOLATOR.

DISC TWO   00:00:00. 01:17:32

TRACK 01   **HAWKWIND** — CITY OF LAGOONS
[IVAN POWELL] PUBLISHED BY ROCK MUSIC PUBLISHING

TRACK 02   **VISNADI** — RACING TRACKS (LE MANS RACE MIX)
[GIANNI VISNADI] COPYRIGHT CONTROL

TRACK 03   **LUISI FANTASIA** — HAPPAMAT KALLOTT
[LUISI FANTASIA] PUBLISHED BY MANUS

TRACK 04   **BOB JAMES** — MOONBOP
[DAVID BROWN] PUBLISHED BY CHELSEA MUSIC PUBLISHING CO LTD

TRACK 05   **THE SALSOUL INVENTION** — SOUL MACHINE (ADDITIONAL EDITS BY DØLLE IØLLEI)
[ANOUDI] PUBLISHED BY SAAR EDIZIONI MUSICALI

TRACK 06   **AXER** — 123
[AXER] PUBLISHED BY EMI MUSIC PUBLISHING / UNIVERSAL MUSIC PUBLISHING

TRACK 07   **DUBARCHANOID TRIM** — PERFUMED GARDEN
[KENZARO IWAKI] PUBLISHED BY SONY ATV

TRACK 08   **MATIAS AGUAYO** — RADIOTAXI
[MATIAS AGUAYO] PUBLISHED BY KOMPAKT MUSICVERLAG

TRACK 09   **RECLOOSE** — CARDIOLOGY (ISOHE MIX)
[MAUK ALSTON] CARDIOLOGICAL MUSIC (BMI) SPANK THAT (BMI)

TRACK 10   **CLOSER MUSIK** — MARIA
[MATIAS AGUAYO, DIRK LEYERS] PUBLISHED BY KOMPAKT MUSICVERLAG

TRACK 11   **ZOMBI** — SAPPHIRE
[STEPHEN MOORE] PUBLISHED BY RELEASE RELAPSE MUSIC (BMI)

TRACK 12   **THE NOW GENERATION** — AFRICAN NIGHTCLUB
[P. LUDEMANN, P. ROJA] PUBLISHED BY COLOURSOUND LIBRARY (GEMA)

TRACK 13   **THE HONEYMOON KILLERS** — DECOLLAGE (PRINS THOMAS MULTITRACK EDIT)
[YVON VROMMAN] PUBLISHED BY CRAMMED MUSIC / STRICTLY CONFIDENTIAL

TRACK 14   **TRES DEMENTED** — SHE'Z SATAN
[CARL CRAIG] PUBLISHED BY PLANET E COMMUNICATIONS /ASCAP

TRACK 15   **MUSICCARGO** — ICH GEH DEN WEG MIT DIR
[GERHARD MICHEL, GORDON POHL] PUBLISHED BY URWALD ORANGE / WARNER CHAPPELL

TRACK 16   **VISNADI** — RACING TRACKS (INDIANAPOLIS DRIVE MIX)
[GIANNI VISNADI] COPYRIGHT CONTROL

TRACK 17   **THE PAPER DOLLS** — GET DOWN BOY (ADDITIONAL EDITS BY LOVE ON THE RUN)
[THE PAPER DOLLS] COPYRIGHT CONTROL

TRACK 18   **PARLIAMENT** — NIGHT OF THE THUMPASORUS PEOPLES
[GEORGE CLINTON JR., WILLIAM EARL COLLINS, GARY MARSHALL SHIDER] PUBLISHED BY BRIDGEPORT MUSIC INC. BMI

Cosmo Galactic Prism Disc Two

LOGAN'S RUN PROMOTIONAL POSTER
Design by Tom Muller

Client: Wear it With Pride (WIWP)
Design firm: Muller
Art direction: Tom Muller
Typography: Tom Muller
Illustration: Tom Muller

This poster design by Muller is an abstract representation of the main themes of the movie *Logan's Run*, including the lifeclock, and the finite cycle of life. As Tom says, the themes of the movie are represented as a circular diagram that tracks the life cycle of the human beings in the movie. Everything, including the protagonists, is contained within this circular pattern, with a few elements extending outside the circle, as happened in the movie.

Muller describes the idea behind his design as that of "transporting the abstract concepts of the movie to a recognizable format. The design is based on the circular pattern to be found in the growth rings of a tree, but it is shown in reverse. The rings in the poster go inward rather than outward to echo the central point of the movie and focus on the plot that drives the whole story."

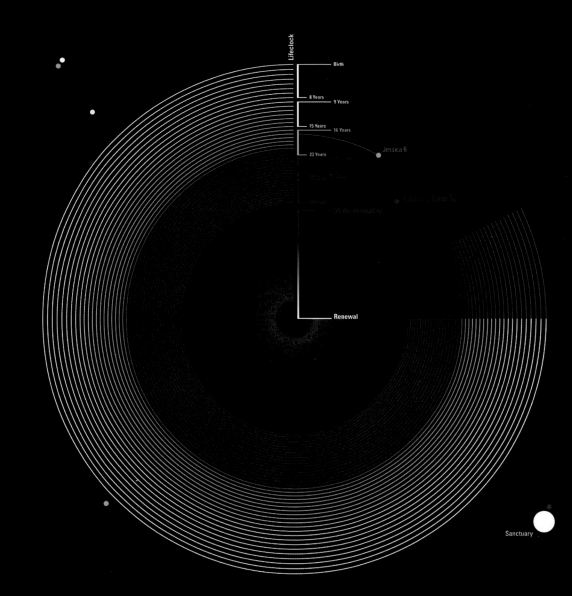

LOGAN'S RUN

METRO-GOLDWYN-MAYER presents A SAUL DAVID PRODUCTION "LOGAN'S RUN" starring MICHAEL YORK – ●JENNY AGUTTER – RICHARD JORDAN – ROSCOE LEE BROWN – FARRAH FAWCETT-MAJORS & PETER USTINOV Screenplay by DAVID ZELAG GOODMAN Based on the novel "LOGAN'S RUN" by WILLIAM F. NOLAN and GEORGE CLAYTON JOHNSON Music – JERRY GOLDSMITH Produced by SAUL DAVID Directed by MICHAEL ANDERSON Filmed in TODD-AO and METROCOLOR poster designed by MULLE

Peter Grundy

Mary Torrieri

Lorenzo Geiger

31Ok

Peter Crnokrak

Pitch Interactive, Inc.

Simon Winter
Dextro

Laurnagaray
Lopez

Rubiera
Ochoa

Statistics

Ivor Williams
Claire Warner

Chris Wilson
Nick Jones

Stephen McGilvray
boing!

Agustin Guerrero
Solana Rey

Marcela Iglesias
Julian Matias Rodriguez

Matt Willey
Matt Curtis

Andy Harvey
Paula Benson

LUST
MAKI

Miriam Ashurst
Chris Griffiths

DEXTRO.ORG ALGORITHMIC IMAGES
Design by Dextro

Client: Self-initiated
Design firm: Dextro.org
Art direction: Dextro
Illustration: Dextro

Dextro takes great pride in using algorithms as the basis for his beautiful and complex images. He uses algorithms to define force fields, subjects objects to these fields, and then intricately plots their paths to create these and other stunning images.

reference

Dextro's diagrams are a visual interpretation of the effect of an algorithm—a sequence of instructions used to make a calculation or process data. In the simplest sense, it is a formula for solving a problem.

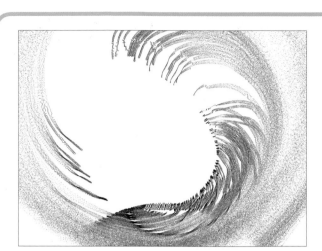

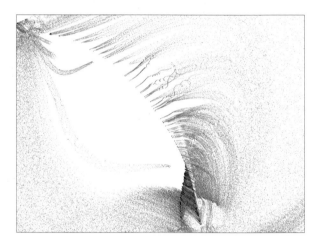

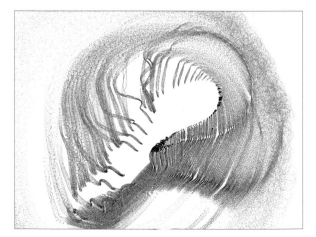

ONCE COMMUNITIES
**Design by Marcela Iglesias,
Solana Rey, Julian Matias Rodriguez,
and Agustin Guerrero**

Client: University of Buenos Aires,
Faculty of Architecture, Design,
and Urbanism

These diagrams explore the ways in which different cultures and groups of people interact in the Once vicinity of Buenos Aires, Argentina. The people are grouped into various categories, including: buyers; the Chinese and Korean communities; the Jewish community; traveling salespeople, who are mostly Peruvian or African-American; wholesalers and retailers; those who collect and deliver goods; and vagrants. Attractive diagrams and tables express such information as which parts of Once particular individuals frequent, how much contact all the groups have with each other, and at what times they have the most and the least interaction. The circular graphics indicate when each section of the commercial population arrives and departs, and defines its peak hours of business. The predominant types of wares are not only listed, but are also linked to certain groups of people and areas of the city.

reference

The designers explain, "Once is one of the cheap markets in Buenos Aires, and part of our design was inspired by cheaply printed items that use single color, dithering, and cheap paper." Consequently, the layout is mostly in black; shading and tints are created through varying patterns of dithering. Although it is difficult to appreciate in this book, the whole piece is printed on cheap paper, rather like newsprint.

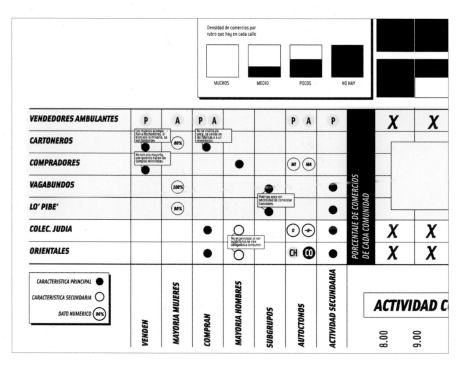

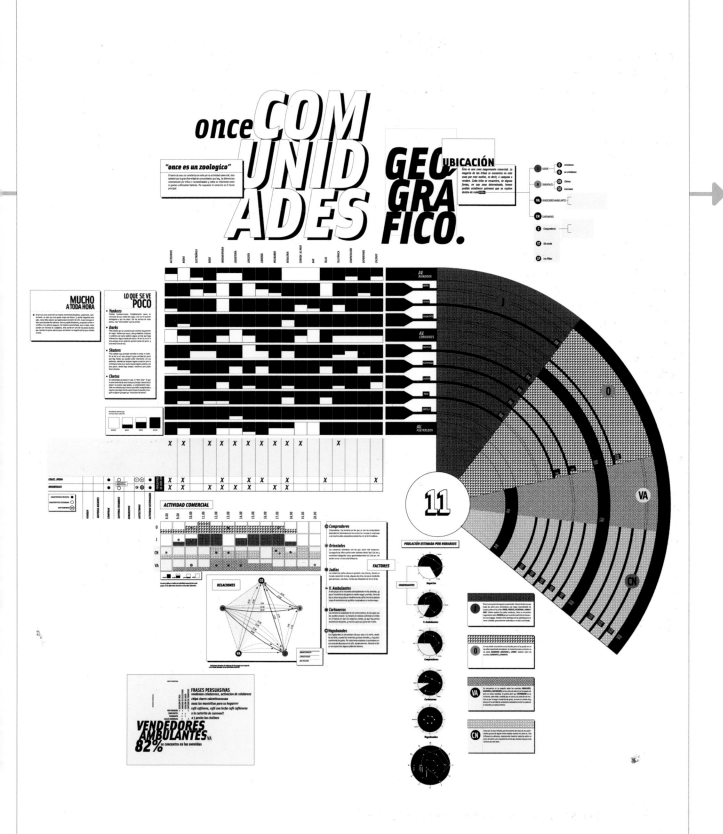

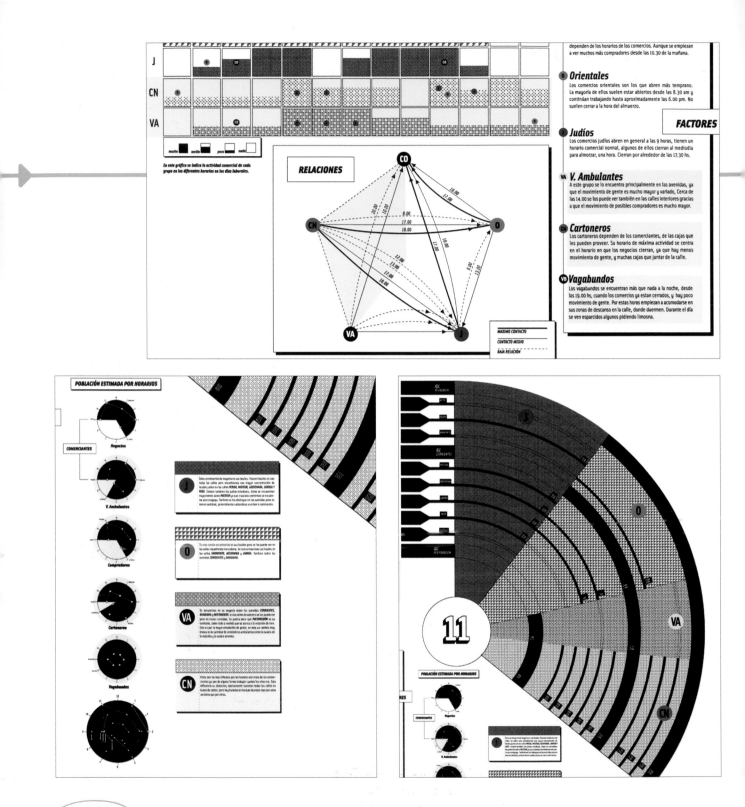

dependen de los horarios de los comercios. Aunque se empiezan a ver muchos más compradores desde las 10.30 de la mañana.

Orientales
Los comercios orientales son los que abren más temprano. La mayoría de ellos suelen estar abiertos desde las 8.30 am y continúan trabajando hasta aproximadamente las 6.00 pm. No suelen cerrar a la hora del almuerzo.

Judíos
Los comercios judíos abren en general a las 9 horas, tienen un horario comercial normal, algunos de ellos cierran al mediodía para almorzar, una hora. Cierran por alrededor de las 17.30 hs.

V. Ambulantes
A este grupo se lo encuentra principalmente en las avenidas, ya que el movimiento de gente es mucho mayor y variado. Cerca de las 14.00 se lo puede ver también en las calles interiores gracias a que el movimiento de posibles compradores es mucho mayor.

Cartoneros
Los cartoneros dependen de los comerciantes, de las cajas que les pueden proveer. Su horario de máxima actividad se centra en el horario en que los negocios cierran, ya que hay menos movimiento de gente, y muchas cajas que juntar de la calle.

Vagabundos
Los vagabundos se encuentran más que nada a la noche, desde las 19.00 hs, cuando los comercios ya están cerrados, y hay poco movimiento de gente. Por estas horas empiezan a acomodarse en sus zonas de descanso en la calle, donde duermen. Durante el día se ven esparcidos algunos pidiendo limosna.

RELACIONES

MÁXIMO CONTACTO
CONTACTO MEDIO
BAJA RELACIÓN

En este gráfico se indica la actividad comercial de cada grupo en los diferentes horarios en los días laborales.

POBLACIÓN ESTIMADA POR HORARIOS

COMERCIANTES

Negocios

V. Ambulantes

Compradores

Cartoneros

Vagabundos

11

DEXTRO.ORG ALGORITHMIC IMAGES
Design by Dextro

Client: Self-initiated
Design firm: Dextro.org
Art direction: Dextro
Illustration: Dextro

Dextro comments that the algorithms themselves are difficult to understand, but that this visual interpretation provides an alternative, and for many a more user-friendly tool for comprehension.

As with the other Dextro designs in this book, this work has taken on a bewitching organic shape, reminiscent of microscopic organisms.

Dextro's fascinating and captivating diagrams are based around his passion for algorithms and his love of problem solving. These designs, like those shown on pages 40 and 41, are detailed visual interpretations of the effects of complex mathematical computations.

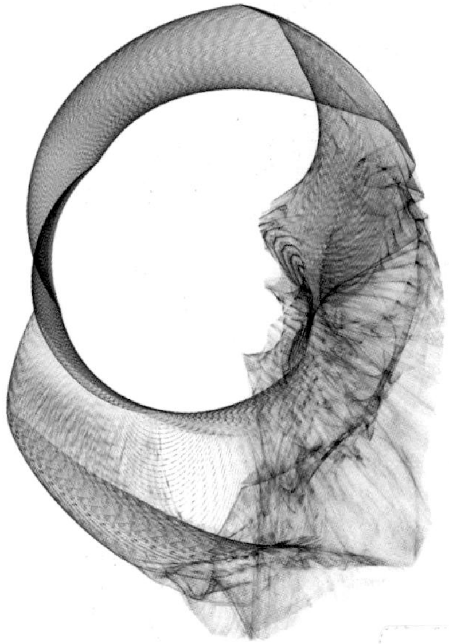

WORLD / SPECTRUM / ARCHIVE
Design by LUST

Client: de Volkskrant
Design firm: LUST

World / Spectrum / Archive is an investigation into the implications of world news viewed at a macro scale. The sum of the current events of a country begins to "speak" of its condition, both domestically and globally. World / Spectrum / Archive approaches this information from a linguistic perspective, evaluating the positive and negative connotations of the headlines of each country, resulting in an image of the state of the world on a given day.

World / Spectrum / Archive pulls five news articles from Google news, from every country in the world, on a daily basis. By comparing ratios of the number of Google search results for a set of positive and negative words, to the ratios of returned results for those words found in the headlines, the program can determine, with 80% accuracy, the semantic orientation of each country, and its headlines. The results are then averaged by country and visualized both geographically and linearly, providing an image of how positive/negative the world is on a given day. The results are also archived, visualizing the shift in each country and its orientation over time. An interesting and unexpected finding of this project is that Western countries tend to be the most positive.

reference

The designers at LUST were clearly inspired by the online news headlines that they have used as the building blocks for this diagrammatic work. By layering brightly colored areas of news, they have been able to create intriguing textural diagrams that, because of the possible levels of interactivity provided by the web, allow an audience to explore the daily comparisons of news data in great detail.

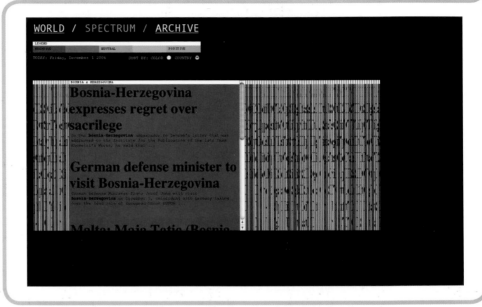

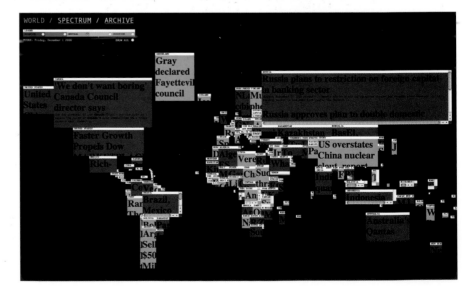

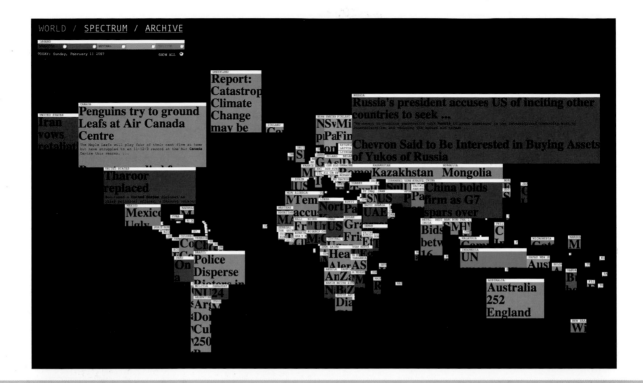

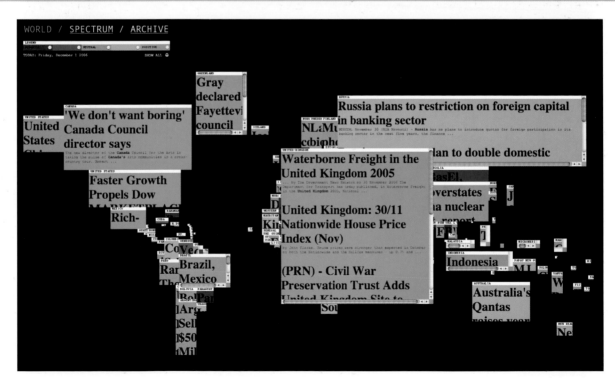

URBAN ATLAS
Design by Laurnagaray, Lopez, Ochoa, and Rubiera

Client: University of Buenos Aires, Faculty of Architecture, Design, and Urbanism

This striking diagram logs information about all the people who use delivery trolleys in their daily routines, within a particular vicinity of Buenos Aires, Argentina. The vocabulary was selected to suggest that the people using the trolleys are in a race. "We are drawing a parallel between car racing and people's lives, while they make use of their trolleys," say the designers.

Certain routes are defined, people are categorized, and obstacles are noted. All observations are made within a set week, and comparisons take into account such aspects as weather conditions, times of day, and frequency of journeys. This diagram captures the excitement and pace of the racetrack.

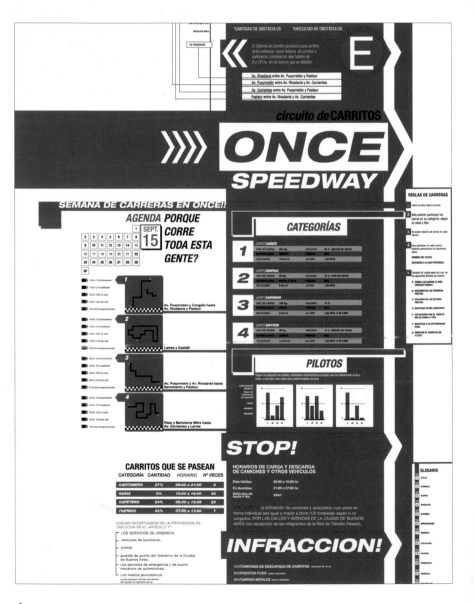

The designers were clearly inspired by the colors and graphics of motor racing: chevrons, coaching lines, checkered flags, arrows, signs, and dashboard dials are all distinctively integrated into every section of the design.

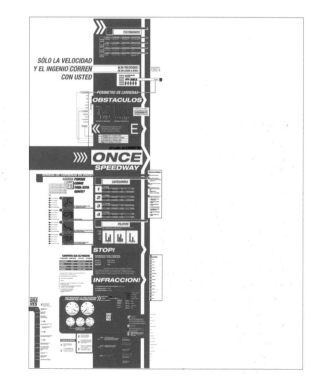

**MARGETING: DESIGN ATLAS
OF GLOBAL SHOES
Design by LUST**

Client: André Plateel
Design firm: LUST

This diagram takes a wall of sports shoes
as its starting point, and examines several
facets of shoe marketing to uncover the
underlying connections between the
brands on display. Details included in
this design include type of shoe, country
of make, market share, wall space and
positioning within the display, advertising
budget, and price. The diagram is a complex
graphic analysis of sports-shoe marketing
strategies, with data gleaned from the
original display wall.

reference

A complex key of colored, lozenge-
shaped lines is used to indicate
details such as brand, country
of origin, and viewing patterns of
shoppers. The individual markings
come together to create separate,
unpredictable diagrams.

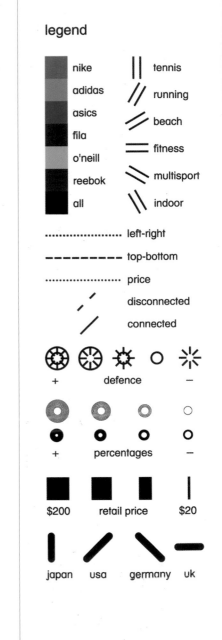

1.01 defence/network/clusters

1.13 wall space vs marketshare: int'l

2.13 retail price vs category

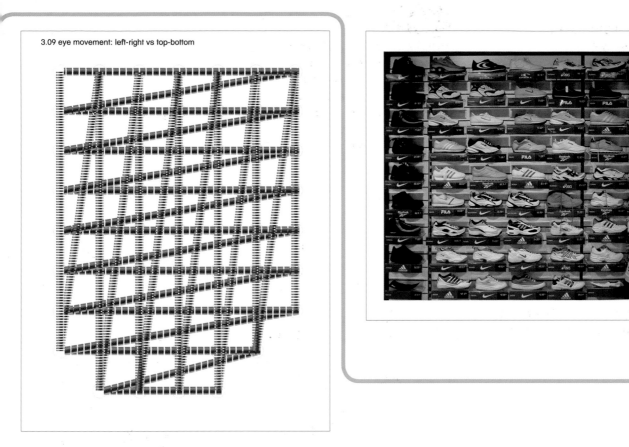

3.09 eye movement: left-right vs top-bottom

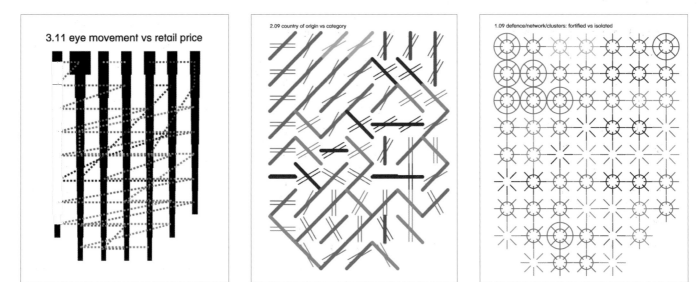

3.11 eye movement vs retail price

2.09 country of origin vs category

1.09 defence/network/clusters: fortified vs isolated

NOORDZEE
Design by LUST

Client: Self-initiated
Design firm: LUST
Art direction: LUST

The North Sea (Noordzee) is a primary focus of many contemporary agendas, including those relating to social and cultural urban issues, and LUST hope that this project will play a significant role in discussions about these issues. For this project, LUST developed a new type of cartography, which they have called "cultural cartography," to represent the sea. They wanted to acknowledge the geographic detail of the area, while focusing on culturally, politically, and commercially significant factors within the North Sea.

LUST show one of the world's most congested seas from 21 different points of view, resulting in 21 distinct thematic maps, including a seafloor map, a city map, a water map, a pollution map, a myth map, and a fear map, among others. Combinations of these maps reveal intriguing commonalities and links. Together with an individual map of the geological area, these combinations create 421 unique maps. "A sea that initially appears empty is revealed to be full—full of the traces of man, such as shipwrecks, cables, pipes, conduits, oil rigs, and so on, and even a massive invasion of monster crabs," says LUST.

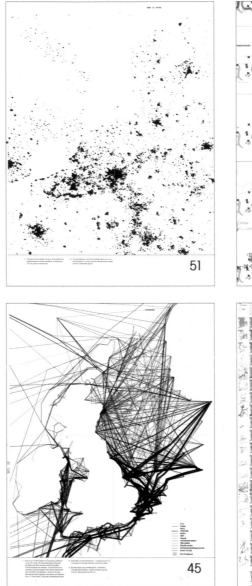

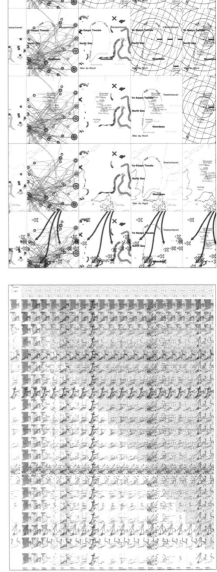

DIAGRAMS: Innovative Solutions for Graphic Designers

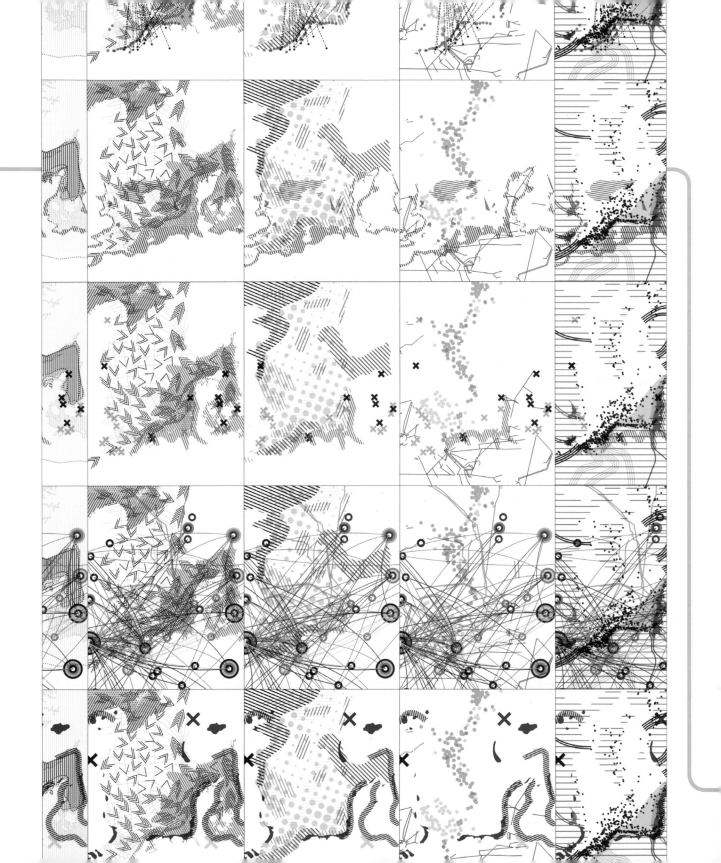

MAPPING:CH AN INVITATION TO FINGER TRAVEL OVER STATISTICALLY MAPPED TERRITORIES
Design by Lorenzo Geiger

Client: Bern University of the Arts
Art direction: Lorenzo Geiger

mapping:ch is a collection of 12 maps, consisting of three main designs and three sets each of smaller detailed pieces that invite the reader to travel through an imaginary statistical landscape of Switzerland. The three main maps—one for researchers and explorers, one with a view to the environment, and one for geographers and analysts—all contain layers of detailed information that is extrapolated to form the three sets of supporting diagrams. Mapping:ch employs a range of complex keys to explain the symbols used in the maps.

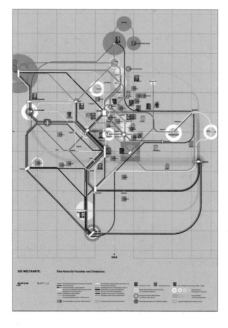

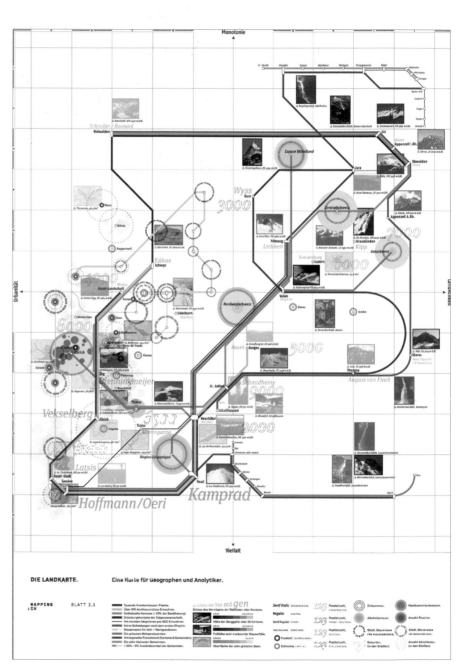

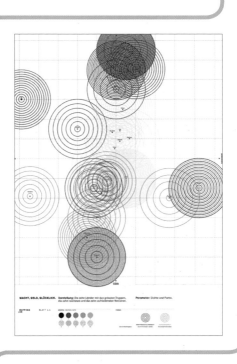

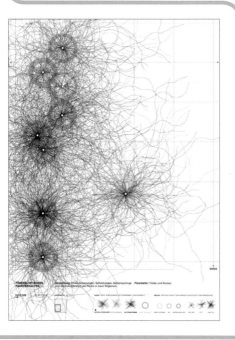

Money makes prosperity

In this diagram, Geiger uses groups of overlapping concentric circles—in cyan, yellow, and magenta—to highlight areas of interest and concentration.

Good hunting

This diagram uses the separations from a number of full-color images of wild animals. Geiger has mixed the dot-screen size for many of these images, but ensured that the reader can easily comprehend the detailed content of the imagery.

National behavior in relationships

This diagram illustrates the number of marriage ceremonies, divorces, affairs, and the satisfaction of couples in nine regions of Switzerland. Geiger uses concentrations of fine, wavy lines in magenta, cyan, and black to define areas of greater or lesser satisfaction with relationships, with some surprising shifts in color emphasis from area to area.

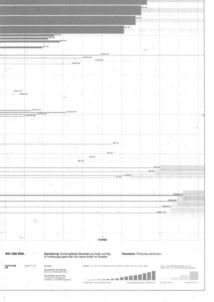

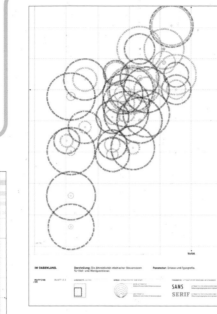

In the oasis land

This example uses circles outlined typographically, using the names of key Swiss locations. Locations shown with cyan serif typography indicate affluent areas; the more prevalent circles framed with black sans-serif place names denote more working-class areas.

There and away

This diagram features a number of complex bar charts that run horizontally across the diagram, from side to side. The bars on the right-hand side are composed of closely packed groups of vertical lines.

Death islands

In this chart, typographic styling is used to identify the prevalence of fatal illnesses in Switzerland.

It is clear that Lorenzo Geiger has drawn inspiration from the highly influential design of the London Underground map by Harry Beck. However, Geiger has included curves in his design, each with the same radius, and varied the width of the lines used.

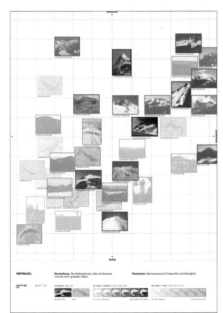

Farsightedness

Small-scale, halftone images of Swiss mountain summits and lakes demonstrate "concentrations of farsightedness."

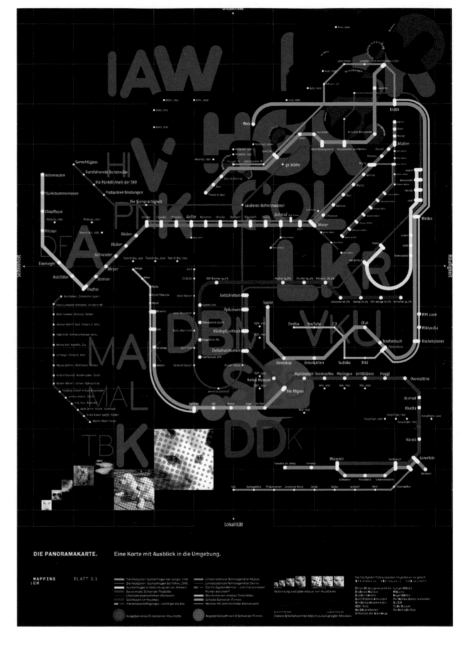

GLOBAL HEADCOUNT
Design by Simon Winter

Client: Self-initiated
Design firm: Simon Winter Design
Art direction: Simon Winter
Typography: Simon Winter

Global Headcount could be interpreted as a world map, a statistical commentary on global population, or a diagrammatic story that links a country's size with its total population.

Simon Winter's design is based on a visual system that was devised to give a clear indication of a country's population in proportion to its land area. Visualizing statistics drawn from CIA figures, each circle represents not only the size and location of a country, but also its population set against its land area. The design is fascinating, and has minimal reliance on written language or statistical data.

The basic unit of Simon's design is the circle, often used for charts, and also to symbolically represent one whole, or 100%.

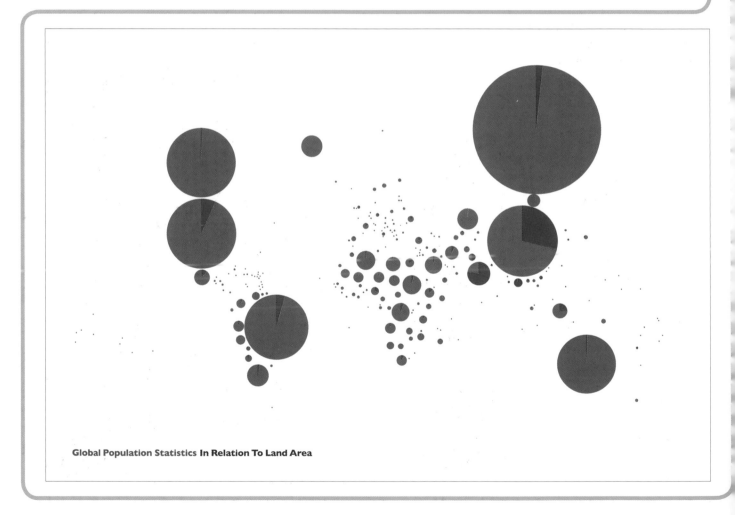

Global Population Statistics In Relation To Land Area

DE PRIJS VAN NEDERLAND
Design by MAKI

Client: FEM Business
Design firm: MAKI
Art direction: MAKI
Illustration: MAKI
Photography: MAKI

MAKI's design for FEM Business shows the general value, in Euros, of the Netherlands' economy. The map itself uses a mix of styles, including distinctive MAKI linework (another example of this style can be seen on pages 16 and 17), collage involving the use of small adhesive price labels, historic portraiture, and background texture.

reference

Old parchment maps and documents were an influence on MAKI for this design. The designers replicated the age of such documents by introducing creases and folds as a subtle background texture, and to break up areas of flat, bright color.

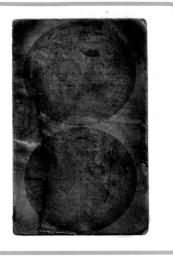

SPAARGELD + PRIVÉBEZIT
€ 1.506.200.000.000

€ 817.500.000.000
ONDERNEMINGEN

€ 1.210.000.000.000
ONROEREND GOED

INFRASTRUCTUUR
€ 508.500.000.000

€ 866.300.000.000
SCHULDEN

€??
KADERS

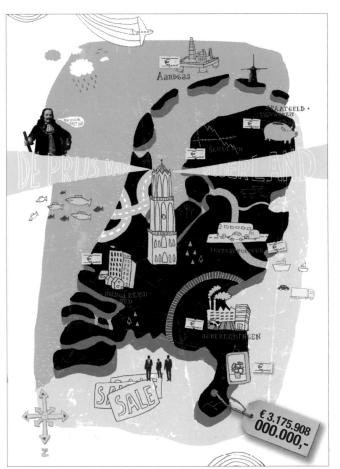

MARKING EUROPE
Design by LUST

Client: Atelier HSL
Design firm: LUST
Art direction: LUST

This unfinished map of Europe gives the impression of an ever-changing union that is always in a state of flux. The map shows that frontiers and borders are constantly evolving, developing, and expanding. LUST's design is based around mapping different concepts of Europe: is it a map of Europe, the Euro, the Eurovision Song contest, the UEFA Cup, or the Europe of corporate logos and brands? "This design is a prototype for a map in a contemporary guise," says LUST. "It will be a digital atlas, an e-book of maps helping the reader to decipher a multilayered landscape of as yet inconceivable journeys, ranging from the routes of overhead power lines, pilgrim trails, and invisible electronic information networks, to the high-speed train routes of tomorrow, and the paths of animal migrations."

The design uses a complex, colorful key: for example, a thick orange line denotes the boundaries of time zones and fine dashed lines plot the routes of Tour De France cycle races. It is reasonably easy to recognize the formation of Europe by focusing on the areas created by concentrations of plotted routes and prospective journeys.

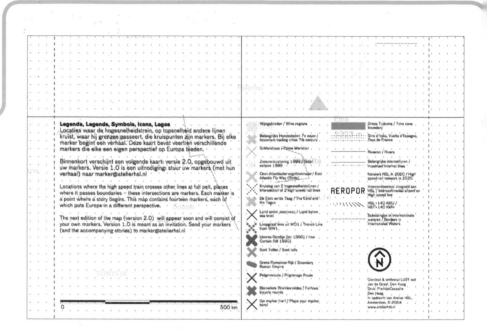

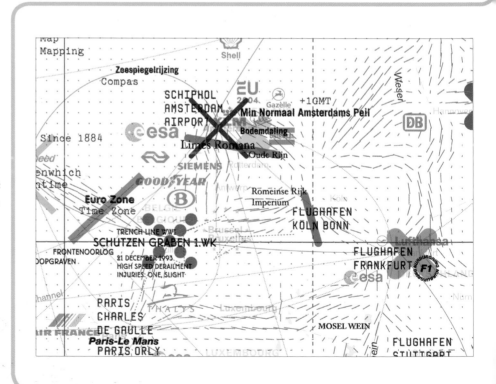

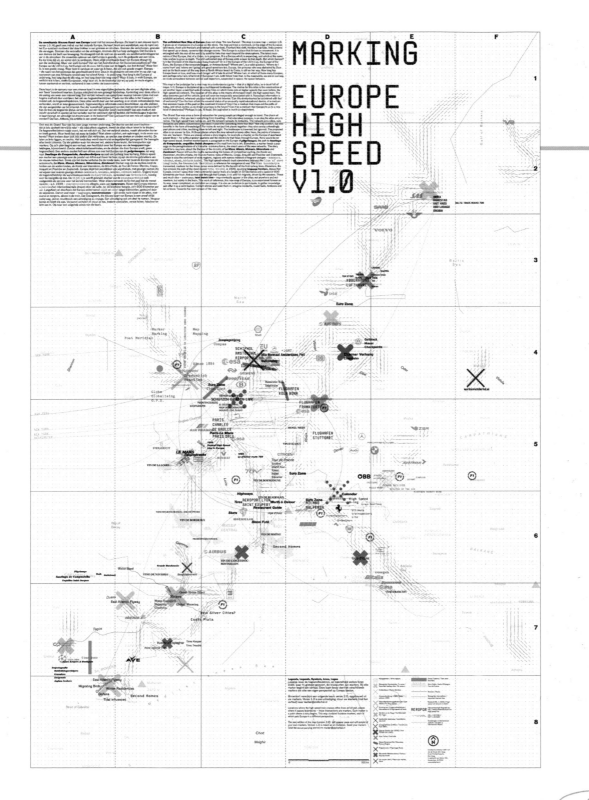

MARKING EUROPE HIGH SPEED V1.0

ARTS & BUSINESS POSTERS
**Design by Andy Harvey
and Paula Benson**

Client: Arts & Business posters
Design firm: Form
Art direction: Paul West
and Paula Benson
Illustration: Andy Harvey

Arts & Business commissioned Form
to enliven the visualization of their
research into private investment in
the arts. Although it is full of facts and
figures, it has been presented in an
accessible way to ensure that audiences
find the maps, charts, and graphs easy
to comprehend.

The map of the United Kingdom has been
dramatically simplified, with the outline
formed only with horizontal, vertical, and
45° lines. Following this, annotations are
also set at 45°. Regions are color-coded,
and 3D detailing is used to represent the
amount of private investment in the arts
within each. The largest investments
were made outside London, in England's
southwest and northeast.

Simple, colorful charts show the total
amount invested in the arts, broken
down into specific art forms. Each
diagram compares the 2004/2005
figures with those of 2005/2006.
The bars are drawn following the same
perspective as that used for the map.
The depth of each bar is built up with
layers of small circles, which provides
a visual link with the final diagram
shown here. This uses overlaid colored
circles to indicate the origin of private
investment in the arts within the region.
It is a fascinating and clever alternative
to the bar chart, showing comparative
investments by setting circles one on
top of the other.

reference

**"The inspiration behind these diagrams
came from the art world, and includes
paint charts and color wheels,"** says
Benson of Form. All of the featured
examples use the same dusky,
contrasting colors.

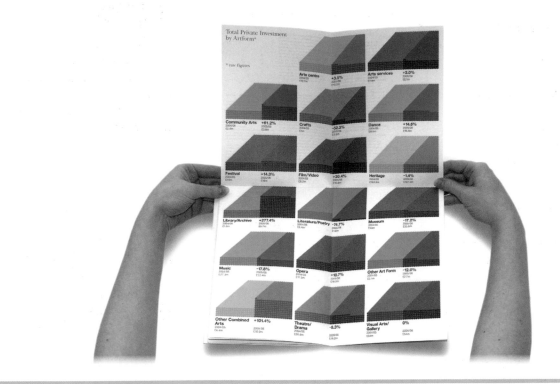

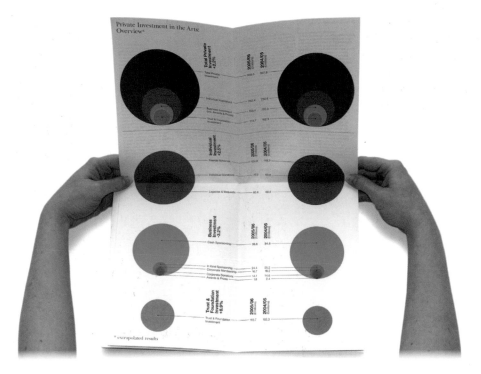

2008 US PRESIDENTIAL CANDIDATE DONATION VISUALIZATION
Design by Pitch Interactive, Inc.

Client: Self-initiated
Design firm: Pitch Interactive, Inc.
Art direction: Wesley Grubbs
Programming: Nick Yahnke

< 100   100 - 500   500 - 1000

These diagrams analyze the donations made to the Obama/McCain US presidential race. They give a fascinating comparison between the amount and origin of money given to the two campaigners. "With thousands of donors for McCain and Obama, we wanted to analyze the types of people giving to each candidate. We examined the top 250 job titles for the supporters of each candidate and tried to determine how much influence they had on the overall donations," says Wesley Grubbs.

On the left side of the arc the job titles are listed left to right, from most common to least common; the right side of the arc is segmented left to right according to cash amounts, from least to most. The job titles are color-coded. With knowledge of the coding used, the reader can quickly interpret the origins and amounts of finances given to each candidate's campaign.

RETIRED
ATTORNEY
NOT EMPLOYED
INFORMATION REQUESTED
PHYSICIAN
PROFESSOR
TEACHER
CONSULTANT
HOMEMAKER
STUDENT
ENGINEER
WRITER
MANAGER
LAWYER
SALES
ARTIST
SOFTWARE ENGINEER
PRESIDENT
CEO
OWNER
EXECUTIVE
PSYCHOLOGIST
ARCHITECT
ACCOUNTANT
ADMINISTRATOR
EDUCATOR
SOCIAL WORKER
REGISTERED NURSE
RN
DIRECTOR
MARKETING
REAL ESTATE
REALTOR
PROJECT MANAGER
EXECUTIVE DIRECTOR
SCIENTIST
EDITOR
ANALYST
OFFICE MANAGER
DESIGNER
BUSINESS OWNER
LIBRARIAN
SOFTWARE DEVELOPER
PSYCHOTHERAPIST
CPA
MUSICIAN
INVESTOR
PROGRAMMER
PHOTOGRAPHER
PARALEGAL
FINANCE
BANKER
GRAPHIC DESIGNER
VICE PRESIDENT
COMPUTER PROGRAMMER
MANAGEMENT CONSULTANT
RESEARCHER
NA
NURSE
DENTIST
ADMINISTRATIVE ASSISTANT
PHARMACIST
LAW PROFESSOR
PROGRAM MANAGER
SELF EMPLOYED
COLLEGE PROFESSOR
SELF
ECONOMIST

reference

It is clear that, even if only on a subliminal level, Pitch Interactive has been influenced by the familiar, graceful form and beautiful color scheme of rainbows.

ANNUAL REPORT 2004
Design by LUST

Client: Mondriaan Foundation
Design firm: LUST
Art direction: LUST

The Mondriaan Foundation was created to stimulate visual arts, design, and the cultural heritage of the Netherlands. Its task is to strengthen the international position of contemporary visual arts and design by offering financial support to enable institutions, companies, and authorities to reach their target audience.

Within this design, a multicolored, three-ring pie chart compares the grants awarded to each project. The colors of each slice of the graph were randomized: red does not always indicate fine arts projects, and blue does not always represent new media. Reinforcing this concept, individual pages of each report are printed on different-colored stock, with the selection randomized during the printing process. Eight different colors were available for the cover, and 20 for the book block. The result of this is that each report is unique, reflecting the artistic and cultural nature of the Mondriaan Foundation.

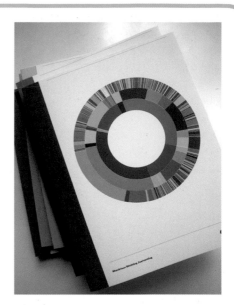

NATIONAL COUNCIL FOR VOLUNTARY ORGANISATIONS (NCVO) ALMANAC
Design by Chris Griffiths and Miriam Ashurst

Client: National Council for Voluntary
Organisations (NCVO)
Design firm: SteersMcGillan Design Ltd.
Art direction: Richard McGillan

The designers have used a distinctive color palette for these forecasting, statistical, and comparative diagrams: rich shades of purple, mustard, green, magenta, and cyan. The most dominant diagram uses a group of transparent colored circles of varying size to represent the amount of overlap between voluntary organizations in civil society. Shapes combine, creating new shades and areas within which to position typographic detail and statistics.

The circular theme continues throughout the diagrams. The designers have used a group of three light gray, closely positioned circles as a background on which to site yellow, green, and magenta circles. The sizes of these colored circles denote the changing patterns within fundraising income generated per UK pound spent.

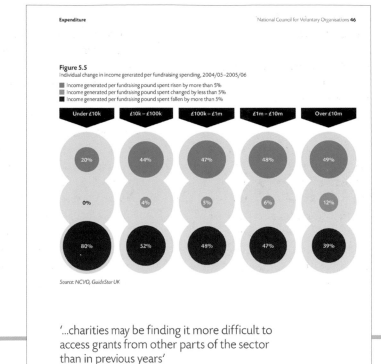

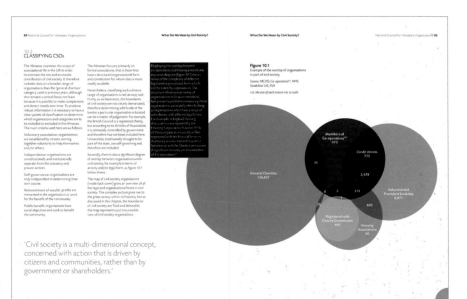

A_B_ PEACE & TERROR ETC.
THE CONCEPTUAL AESTHETICS
OF LOVE AND HATE
Design by Peter Crnokrak

Client: Design Supremo
Design firm: The Luxury of Protest
Art direction: Peter Crnokrak
Illustration: Peter Crnokrak

A_B_peace & terror etc. is a geopolitical survey of the 192 member States of the United Nations. It concerns the quantitative degree to which each state contributes to peace and terror in the world. This screen-printed poster is double-sided, with the A-side showing survey results concerning peace, printed black; and the B-side showing results concerning terror, printed gray on a semitranslucent paper stock.

The double-sided nature of the poster is highly functional in that it allows for an instant visual comparison of data relating to both peace and terror. On each side the graph is divided into three rings, giving three separate indexes for peace and three separate indexes for terror. These rings are individual quantitative measures obtained from researchers working on geopolitical issues.

The quantitative variation for the peace and terror measures is represented through differences in line thickness. For example, a line width of 1pt denotes a low value, and 10pt a high value.

The inner ring of the A side conveys information from the Global Peace Index, and ranks countries by their absence of violence, using metrics that combine both internal and external factors that contribute to peace. The middle ring on this side details the Happy Planet Index, and quantifies the ecological efficiency with which human well-being is delivered. The final, outer ring represents well-being; this index is a measure of the underlying state of happiness and satisfaction with life, in both general and specific terms.

On the B side, the inner ring conveys information about the Political Terror Scale. It represents a numerical measure of each State's political violence and human rights violations. The middle ring speaks of weapons holdings per capita, and is an estimated measure of the national per-capita holdings of light and heavy military, paramilitary, law enforcement, and civilian weapons. Lastly, the outer ring charts military

expenditure per capita, which is derived from the NATO definition: all current and capital expenditures on the armed forces, including peacekeeping forces, defense ministries and other government agencies engaged in defense projects, paramilitary forces, and military space activities.

FACTS AND FIGURES FOR AMSTERDAM INDEX ANNUAL
Design by 310k

Client: Bis Publishers
Design firm: 310k
Art direction: 310k
Typography: 310k
Illustration: 310k

The facts and figures section of the Amsterdam Index is all about envisioning information concerning the creation and benefits of the establishment of a creative city. Design firm 310k used a mix of charts, tables, and graphs to communicate the statistical results of the research.

At a glance, the reader can see the recent increases in the creative jobs market in Amsterdam and the surrounding areas, and also, thanks to clearly set out tabular design, the knock-on benefits to the economy of the region.

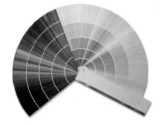

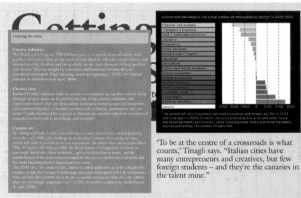

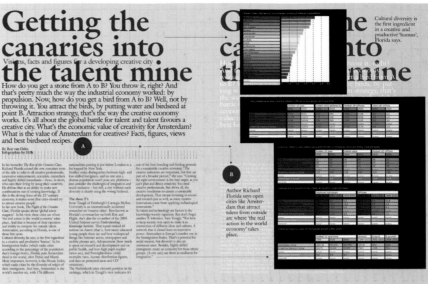

Getting the canaries into the talent mine

Visions, facts and figures for a developing creative city

How do you get a stone from A to B? You throw it, right? And that's pretty much the way the industrial economy worked: by propulsion. Now, how do you get a bird from A to B? Well, not by throwing it. You attract the birds, by putting water and birdseed at point B. Attraction strategy, that's the way the creative economy works. It's all about the global battle for talent and talent favours a creative city. What's the economic value of creativity for Amsterdam? What is the value of Amsterdam for creatives? Facts, figures, views and best birdseed recipes.

By Roy van Dalm
Infographics by 310k

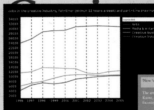

A

In his bestseller *The Rise of the Creative Class*, Richard Florida coined the new container term of the title to refer to all creative professionals, innovative entrepreneurs, scientists, researchers and highly skilled consultants – those, in short, who earn their living by using their creativity. He defines that as an ability to make new combinations out of existing knowledge. If this is the driving force of the 21st-century economy, it makes sense that cities should try to attract creative people.
In his new book, *The Flight of the Creative Class*, Florida speaks about 'global talent magnets'. In his view, these cities are where 'the real action in the world economy' takes place. And that is because of their openness and ability to compete for outside talent. Amsterdam, according to Florida, is one of these hot spots.
Cultural diversity, he says, is the first ingredient in a creative and productive 'humus'. In his Immigration Index (which ranks cities according to the percentage of the population that's foreign-born), Florida puts Amsterdam third in the world, after Dubai and Miami. More important, however, is the Mosaic Index, which ranks cities by the diversity of origin of their immigrants. And here, Amsterdam is the world's number six, with 174 different

nationalities putting it just below London to a key topped by New York.
Neither index distinguishes between high- and low-skilled foreigners, and no one says a diverse population won't pose any problems – just consider the challenges of integration and social exclusion – but still, a city without such diversity is clearly using the wrong birdseed.

The three T's
Irene Tinagli of Pittsburgh's Carnegie Mellon University is an internationally acclaimed researcher on 'creative cities'. Best known is Florida's crosswalker on both Rise and Flight, she's also the co-author of the 2003 United Nations survey *Understanding Knowledge Societies*. That report ranked 45 nations on Amets (that is, how more educated young people fare and how widespread things like Internet access, newspapers and mobile phones are). Advancement (how much is spent on research and development and on public health, and how high pupil-teacher ratios are), and Foresightedness (child mortality rates, income distribution figures, and data on protected areas and CO2 emissions).
The Netherlands takes eleventh position in the rankings, which in Tinagli's view indicates it's

one of the best breeding and feeding grounds for a sustainable creative economy. The creative industries are important, but they are part of a broader picture," she says. "Creating the right environment is the best target, as you can't plan and direct creativity. You need creative professionals, but above all, the creative conditions to create a sustainable development. That means investing in science and research just as well, as many creative innovations come from applying technological innovations."
So talent and technology are factors in the knowledge-society equation. But don't forget number T: tolerance. Says Tinagli, "You have to keep society very open to make it an intersection of different ideas and cultures. A network that is closed loses its innovative power. Amsterdam is Europe's number one in the Immigration Index. That's a potential for social tension, but diversity is also an enormous asset. Besides, highly skilled immigrants create an economy for those ethnic groups. [A city can] use them as mediators for integration."

B

Author Richard Florida says open cities like Amsterdam are where 'the real action in the world economy' takes place.

Getting the

Finally, the city council says in a strategy document that its cultural policy over the next decade will be geared toward making Amsterdam a place where "all meet all in an interaction involving people from widely different backgrounds, culture belongs to the Amsterdammers, and art and culture have a solid economic foundation." In other words, the city should be a socially inclusive mosaic with committed citizens and economically solid creative industries. There's a strong emphasis on the concept of 'shareholdership', meaning the government wants to encourage people to feel like co-owners of the city by getting them involved in cultural activities. Yet it has to be said that its recent decision to slash arts subsidies by 3 million euros over the next three years isn't very conducive to promoting cultural inclusion.

Where it's (going to be) at
The city centre is the heart of the creative industries. Hemel says this is surprising proof that the area "is not a monofunctional, tourist and consumption paradise." More striking is the fact that the vast majority of such businesses are one-person firms. Few exceed a staff of 20 people. "Amsterdam is a city of creative freelancers, working in temporary networks and clusters, preferring to stay independent," says Hemel. "Sixty percent of all creative-industry activities are carried out from home."
The question that most tickles the imagination of Amsterdam policymakers is: where will these free birds move next to feed? "Can we create or at least promote the quality of the places where it should all be happening next?" Hemel says. Certain movements are already visible. The 19th-century houses in the old southern part of the city were the habitat of lawyers and accountants and the like; now he sees those professionals moving out to the new office developments of Zuidas, with creatives moving in to take their places. Meanwhile, the new urban population is taking up residence in the eastern docklands. And creative-industry pioneers, like MTV Networks and dance-music promoters and publishers ID&T, which usually require lots of space, are settling in the north. "Noord, Buiksloterdam and the NDSM wharf area may well become the new creative hot spots," Hemel says. "We also have high hopes for the Overamstel area, near the Amstel railway station. The present industries there are disappearing, and we want to restructure this huge area for mixed residential and commercial development." Then there is a part of the creative industries that really wants to move into the western docklands. The city's port authority has been against it, but the [harbour basin] Minervahaven already has an

architectural firm and a film studio. All in all, the spatial demands of the creative industries are more than catered for."

A cosmopolitan village
In researcher Harry Grosveld's 2002 survey of 1,300 of the world's most prominent 'city makers' –public and private institutions that contribute to a city's image, from art and tourism organisations to real-estate traders and universities – Amsterdam came in twelfth in terms of how well it was generally perceived. For quality of trade, transport and museums, it was ranked sixth. Yet if the city wants to keep that international appeal, it will probably have to do even more: attract visitors and foreign talent, keep improving cultural amenities and all sorts of business accommodation, keep housing affordable, solve tensions between ethnic groups, and generally stay safe and accessible.
To keep up, the city will have to map the new creative landscape onto the policies of the economic, culture, and spatial planning departments. It's working on that: Robert Marijnissen, the city's programme manager for the creative industries, says, "Co-operation between departments and with [the city marketing organisation] Amsterdam Partners has resulted in Amsterdam International Fashion Week and Inside Design, an event showing the latest developments in interior-product design." The city's economic and cultural departments also run a project that combines training in entrepreneurial skills, the supplying of working and living accommodation, assistance with microfinance, and a web portal for the creative industries, Marijnissen says. "And the cultural department is putting money into a project that brings pre-vocational schools and creative industries together." Crossover is the key word. The Amsterdam

Creativity Exchange (ACX), a networking organisation for the creative industries and the business sector, is an example. Michiel Schwarz, a consultant on technology and culture and a member of the national Council for Culture, researches crossover projects like these, and the intersections between technology, culture, media and the economy in general. "You need crossover projects," he says. "Innovation comes from overlapping areas that will, in turn, become new core areas. It's about crossing fashion with media, or media with education. Why not ask a creative new-media company to develop an educational game or design a museum display?" As an example he cites Frequency 1550, a game that allows children to explore the city's history using new UMTS technology. It is a joint project of the new-media research and development organisation Waag Society, the telecom company KPN, and a primary school.
To Schwarz, fostering creativity in a city is about "designing and facilitating the nodes in the network." He says, "It's the physical and virtual nodes where people and products meet that are the crossovers of innovation. So a city needs people who can work at the crossroads of disciplines. The advantage of Amsterdam in this respect is its compact size. It is a cosmopolitan village with short links between nodes. That makes it easier to stimulate new developments."

Lawyers and accountants are moving into Zuidas and out of the old south side; creatives are moving in to take their places. The new urban population is going to the eastern docklands, and companies like MTV Networks are settling in the north.

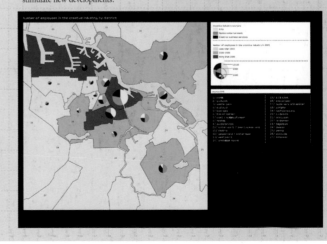

A city needs people who can work at the crossroads of disciplines. Amsterdam is a cosmopolitan village with short links between nodes; that makes it easier to stimulate new developments."

HISCOX LTD. REPORT AND ACCOUNTS 2007
Design by Claire Warner and Ivor Williams

Client: Hiscox
Design firm: Browns
Art direction: Jonathan Ellery

"Hiscox's chairman asked Browns to design an annual report that 'told it how it is.' This had to be a bold, no-nonsense document," says Jonathan Ellery. Graphs and charts are, for the most part, set against a black background which emphasizes the statistical information.

The graph entitled Building a Balanced Business is actually four graphs in one; the gross premiums of four separate areas of Hiscox business are shown overlaid, with the whole still providing easily accessible, discrete information.

This report also features a number of very simple, yet powerful pie charts. Each slice is annotated simply with small-print, sans-serif text.

The Boxplot and whisker diagram explains Hiscox's net loss. It provides details of the industry loss return period, and of variability in expected industry loss. The diagram is also annotated to inform the reader of the causes of some of these significant losses. For example, Hurricane Katrina caused an estimated $39 billion market loss that will have an 18-year return period.

The solution was inspired by the tone and color of the stock used by London's *Financial Times*.

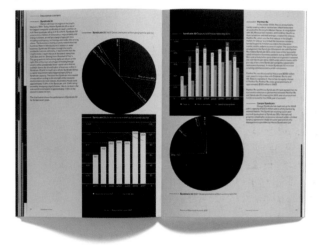

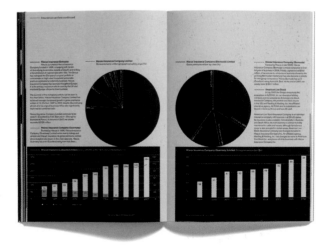

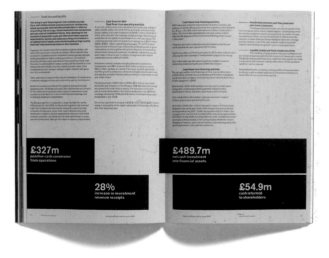

GREATER PHILADELPHIA CULTURAL ALLIANCE 2008 PORTFOLIO
Design by Mary Torrieri

Client: Greater Philadelphia
    Cultural Alliance
Design firm: Joel Katz Design Associates
Art direction: Joel Katz

This diagram was created to indicate the attendance levels at various categories of cultural event in the Philadelphia area, in Pennsylvania, USA. This graph is just one of over 30 that were produced for the Philadelphia Cultural Alliance's second biannual report, covering the health of the cultural institutions in the area. "Every graph in our report has a form appropriate to its subject," comments Katz.

reference

"This graph was inspired by the circular form of an auditorium seating plan," Katz explains. Taking inspiration from this source allowed him to use the "virtual" positioning of seating rows as a graph. For example, attendance at dance performances was 335,000, which is shown by a curved purple block extending over just three virtual seating rows.

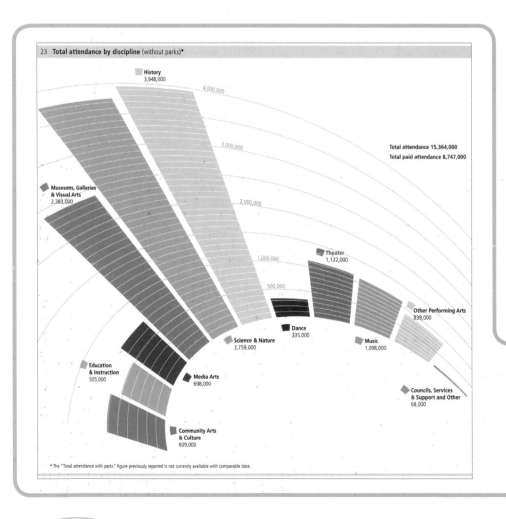

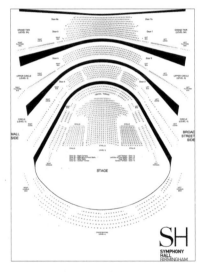

IN THE BLACK
Design by Stephen McGilvray

Client: The Climate Group
Design firm: Browns
Art direction: Nick Jones
Illustration: Lucy Vigrass (Peepshow)

Browns used simple graphs and charts to illustrate the complex facts surrounding the rapid growth experienced by companies providing innovative low-carbon products and services. Weighty horizontals and verticals create the basic axes, while dominant red bars and ascending rules plot the paths of complex data in a highly visible manner.

reference

The name of this project, In The Black, provided the inspiration for Browns' design approach. Browns reversed each diagram through a solid black background, using the contrast between this dark color and the light gray and white horizontal stripes that make up the body of each diagram, to focus the reader's attention on complex matters.

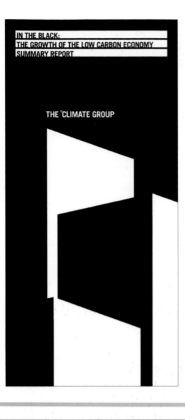

IN THE BLACK:
THE GROWTH OF THE LOW CARBON ECONOMY
SUMMARY REPORT

THE °CLIMATE GROUP

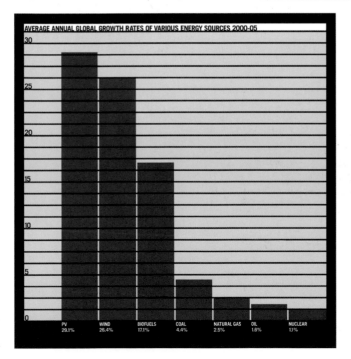

AVERAGE ANNUAL GLOBAL GROWTH RATES OF VARIOUS ENERGY SOURCES 2000-05

| PV | WIND | BIOFUELS | COAL | NATURAL GAS | OIL | NUCLEAR |
| 29.1% | 26.4% | 17.1% | 4.4% | 2.5% | 1.6% | 1.1% |

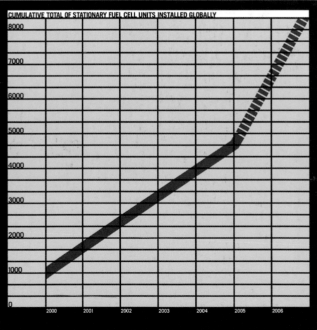

CUMULATIVE TOTAL OF STATIONARY FUEL CELL UNITS INSTALLED GLOBALLY

HAMPTON COURT FOOD CONSUMPTION DIAGRAM
Design by Peter Grundy

Client: Studio 8 Design for Hampton Court Palace
Design firm: Grundini Ltd.
Typography: Peter Grundy
Illustration: Peter Grundy

The information in this diagram could easily be communicated through a simple table, however, Grundy chose to use simple illustration and typography to communicate these surprising figures in a highly amusing way.

 reference

In 1536 Hans Holbein painted a portrait of Henry VIII; his striking painting provided the inspiration behind this diagram depicting the amount of food consumed annually by Henry's court at Hampton Court Palace, near London. Holbein gave his Henry VIII a noticeably square head and wide neck, and it is these two features that have provided the undoubted humor in Peter Grundy's design.

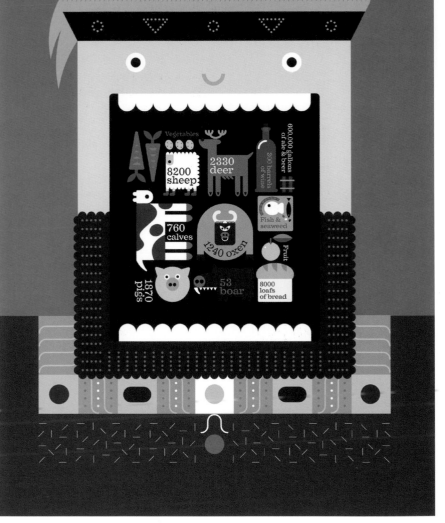

2008 US PRESIDENTIAL CANDIDATE DONATION VISUALIZATION
Design by Pitch Interactive, Inc.

Client: Self-initiated
Design firm: Pitch Interactive, Inc.
Art direction: Wesley Grubbs
Programming: Nick Yahnke

This diagram is the first visualization plotting the level and origin of public donations to the candidates involved in the 2008 US presidential race. The second version can be seen on pages 64 and 65. In this "flower" diagram the black, hair-like lines extending from the edges of the design are actually the names of each donor.

Pitch Interactive feel that the density of these names provides a useful visual reference to the size of the donations. The actual segments themselves are categories of donation. Of the petals, the outermost section represents donations between $1 and $100, the middle section donations between $101 and $500, and the inner section donations between $501 and $1,000. The center of the flower represents donations over $1,000.

The second version can be seen on pages 64 and 65.

reference

When asked what motivated them to produce this captivating diagram, Wesley replied, "As nerdy as it sounds, the data was our biggest inspiration." It was the thrill of dealing with large amounts of complex data and waiting for the totally unexpected surprise of the resulting visual; of representing such a heated topic in a clear, objective, and indisputable form.

NORTHSOUTHEASTWEST
Design by Nick Jones and Chris Wilson

Client: The Climate Group
Design firm: Browns
Art direction: Nick Jones
Photography: Magnum

This publication is aimed at prime
ministers, chairmen, and CEOs.
It provides a comprehensive review
of climate change, covering issues, key
happenings, and possible solutions.

Color and central positioning are used
to heighten the impact of these facts;
each beautifully drawn graph, diagram,
or map simply uses white or red to

contrast with the black backgrounds.
Commenting on the distinctive design
approach, Nick Jones of Browns explains,
"Design-wise, we felt it should feel
scientific, yet retain a contemporary
edge, hence the red, black, and white,
combined with angled delivery."

reference

The inspiration for NorthSouthEastWest
came from a combination of sources,
including the *National Geographic*
magazine, and an atlas of the world.

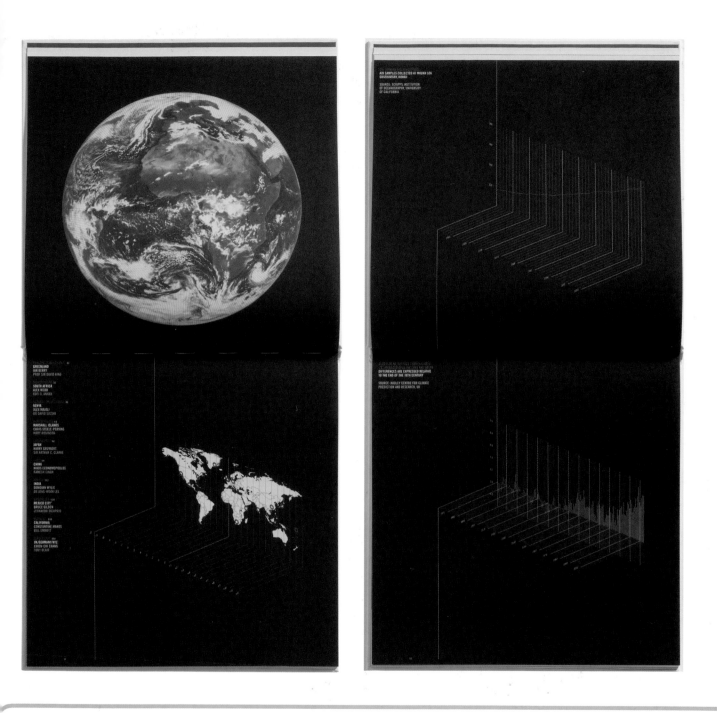

WORLD OF VIOLENCE
Design by Lorenzo Geiger

Client: Bern University of the Arts
Art direction: Lorenzo Geiger

This fascinating, but somewhat alarming design records, by means of color blocks, the area of the front page of Switzerland's regional newspaper, *Der Bund*, that has been devoted to reports of aggression and violence over a continuous period of 64 days.

A solid red shape is substituted for each such report. The resulting design plots the fluctuation in reports of violence during this time period. Alarmingly, there appears to be only one violence-free day.

«The ‹Up & Down› of violence in our daily newspaper»

FUTU MAGAZINE, "LABELS"
Design by Matt Willey and Matt Curtis

Client: Publishing and Design Group Ltd.
Design firm: Studio8 Design
Art direction: Matt Willey

The theme of the sixth issue of *Futu Magazine* was labels, "which in reality means brands," says designer Matt Willey. Studio8 created five separate charts, each of which shows the value, in US dollars, of 10 individual brands.

The charts are color-coded, helping to divide them into the separate business sectors of apparel, technology, fast food, soft drinks, and cars. Each chart is shown in a different perspective, and the resulting imagery has a monolithic, sculptural quality that would not be out of place in an art gallery. The color bars of each design contrast dynamically with their solid silver background.

The inspiration for these designs came from the building industry and, in particular, the 3D programs used to help architects visualize their ideas. In this case, Studio8 experimented with Google's free visualization software SketchUp, which allowed them to create simple 3D shapes that are geometrically correct and also correctly shown in varied perspective.

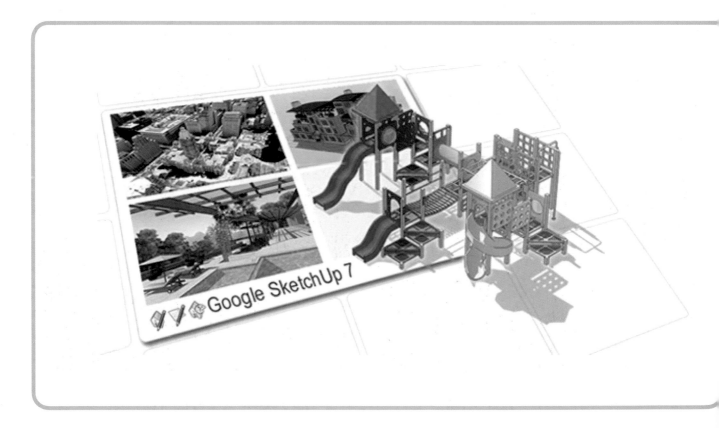

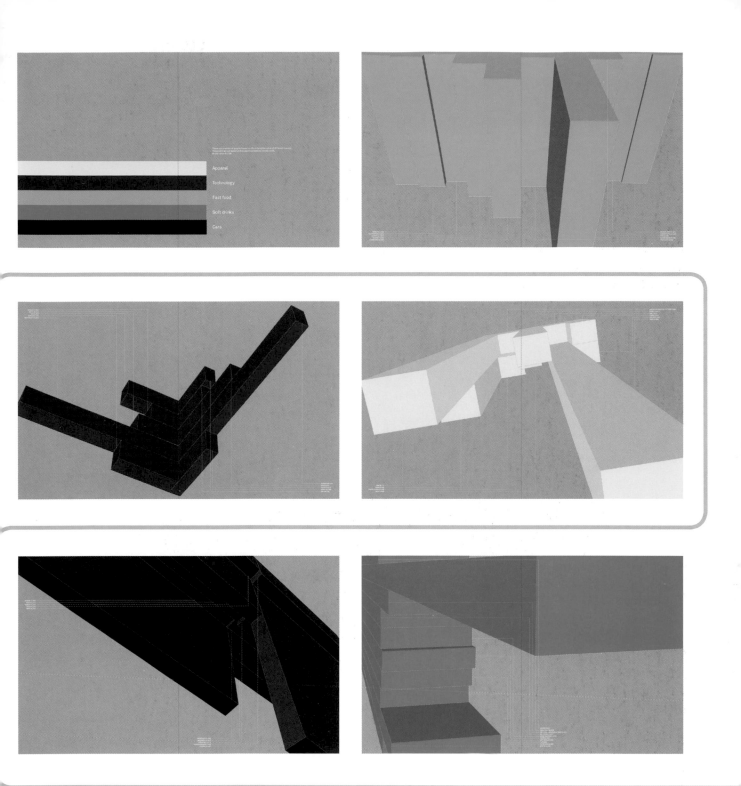

G2 RUBBISH GRAPHIC
Design by Peter Grundy

Client: The *Guardian*
Design firm: Grundini Ltd.
Typography: Peter Grundy
Illustration: Peter Grundy

Peter Grundy's design for the *Guardian* uses a range of charts and tables set within the Keep Britain Tidy symbol to explain how much domestic and commercial waste is being produced, and how this is being dealt with.

The upper part of the figure is used to accommodate two different types of chart. The first diagram is a pie chart, in the form of a stylized garbage sack, showing how waste is processed in England and Wales. The second plots the surprising increase in the export of wastepaper and cardboard from the UK between 1980 and 2004.

Rubbish

From household garbage to industrial waste, we are producing ever more rubbish. But just how big a problem is it? And how are we dealing with it?

3 What happens our waste?

The g2 graphic

● **Fly-tipping costs around £150m** each year to clear up

● **The area of land in England and Wales used for landfill sites is about 28,000 hectares—0.2%** of the total land area

● **In 2004, 72%** of newsprint was made from recycled paper, compared to 26.2% in 1990

● **Around 20%** of the food we buy is discarded, meaning that on average every household throws away £424 of wasted food each year

1 How much do we throw away?

● The average Briton now produces around 520kg of household waste each year – roughly seven times the average body weight. In 1983, we each threw away 397kg a year

Per capita municipal waste, by region

	(Kg)
East	539
South East	560
West Midlands	570
South West	573
East Midlands	575
Yorkshire & the Humber	585
London	595
Northern Ireland	600
Wales	620
North West	644
North East	645
Scotland	660

Annual per capita municipal waste output, by country

	% change
US	-1.0
Germany	+14.4
France	+8.9
England	+18.2
Japan	+1.0

800kg / 700kg / 600kg / 500kg / 400kg / 300kg per capita

1995   2001

2 What do we throw away?

● For every tonne of household waste we produce, commercial, industrial and construction businesses produce another sh...

Total annual waste, by sector, 2002/3

Other 5.1%
Construction Demolition
Household 9.3%
Commercial 10.5%
Industrial 13.5%
Mining Quarry 28.7%
Other: Agriculture, sewage and dredged material

● Retail packaging ac... for about 40% of household wa...

Household waste, by type

Garden Waste 20%
Paper and Board 18%
Kitchen Waste 17%
General Household Sweepings 9%

Glass 7%
Scrap metal
White good
Wood 5%
Dense plast
Plastic film
Textiles 3%
Metal packaging
Soil 3%
Nappies 2%

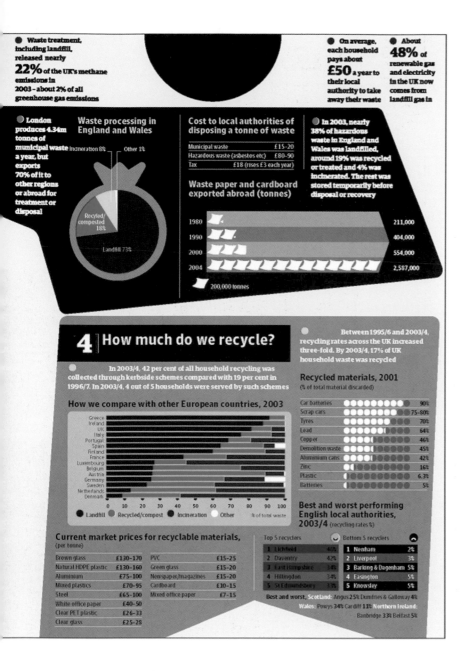

The lower section of the Keep Britain Tidy figure contains a number of complex graphs. The largest and most dominant uses the overlay of colored bars to indicate how the UK's treatment of waste compares with other European countries. The second diagram compares the amount of materials discarded to the amount recycled in 2001.

More diagrams are found within the trashcan. Two use simplified images of trashcans, filled to different levels to indicate the composition of household waste, and the annual per capita municipal waste per country.

G2 THE ARMS TRADE GRAPHIC
Design by Peter Grundy

Client: The *Guardian*
Design firm: Grundini Ltd.
Typography: Peter Grundy
Illustration: Peter Grundy

The human cost and limited financial benefits of the arms trade are weighed up in this diagram. Five characterful, simplified illustrations of military hardware are used to contain graphs, charts, and a map that provide the reader with the uncomfortable details relating to the arms trade.

A khaki warship contains a graph that details arms exports to a number of leading countries. The bars within this graph are designed to resemble torpedoes.

A simplified illustration of a hand grenade is used as the background to a color-coded, annotated map of the world, plotting the countries to which Britain sells arms. A bright green tank features a number of charts that show Peter Grundy's characteristic use of repetition: this time iconic purple shells and small "explosions." Each symbol has a direct relevance to the subject matter being explored.

The final section of this diagram features two large stylized bombs that are the backdrop for charts and graphs.

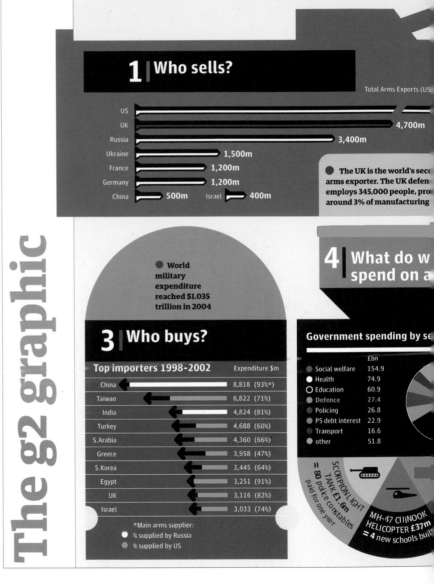

Each week the Guardian's Leo Hickman and award-winning information design agency Grundy Northedge collaborate on a unique in-depth graphic providing an instant briefing on one of the issues of the week

The arms trade

This week leading weapons manufacturers gather in London for one of the world's largest arms fairs. The global industry in now worth $1 trillion a year, but who benefits from this trade and what is the human cost?

1 | Who sells?

Total Arms Exports (US

US	
UK	4,700m
Russia	3,400m
Ukraine	1,500m
France	1,200m
Germany	1,200m
China	500m Israel 400m

● The UK is the world's seco arms exporter. The UK defen employs 345,000 people, pro around 3% of manufacturing

● World military expenditure reached $1.035 trillion in 2004

3 | Who buys?

Top importers 1998-2002　　Expenditure $m

China	8,818 (93%*)
Taiwan	6,822 (71%)
India	4,824 (81%)
Turkey	4,688 (60%)
S.Arabia	4,360 (66%)
Greece	3,958 (47%)
S.Korea	3,445 (64%)
Egypt	3,251 (91%)
UK	3,116 (82%)
Israel	3,033 (74%)

*Main arms supplier:
○ % supplied by Russia
● % supplied by US

4 | What do w spend on a

Government spending by se

	£bn
● Social welfare	154.9
● Health	74.9
○ Education	60.9
● Defence	27.4
● Policing	26.8
● PS debt interest	22.9
● Transport	16.6
● other	51.8

SCORPION LIGHT TANK £1.6m = 80 police constables paid for one year

MH-47 CHINOOK HELICOPTER £37m = 4 new schools buil

The g2 graphic

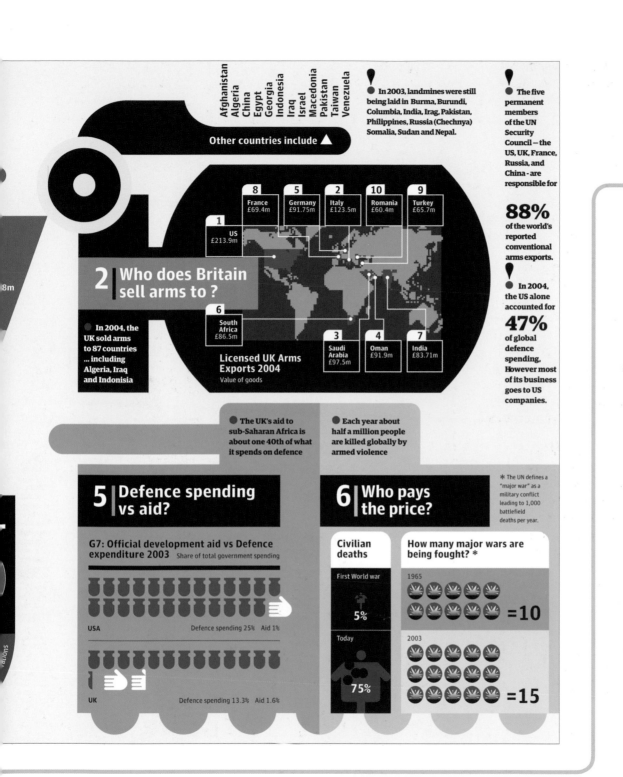

Afghanistan
Algeria
China
Egypt
Georgia
Indonesia
Iraq
Israel
Macedonia
Pakistan
Taiwan
Venezuela

Other countries include ▲

● In 2003, landmines were still being laid in Burma, Burundi, Columbia, India, Iraq, Pakistan, Philippines, Russia (Chechnya) Somalia, Sudan and Nepal.

● The five permanent members of the UN Security Council — the US, UK, France, Russia, and China - are responsible for

88%

of the world's reported conventional arms exports.

● In 2004, the US alone accounted for

47%

of global defence spending, However most of its business goes to US companies.

8	France £69.4m
5	Germany £91.75m
2	Italy £123.5m
10	Romania £60.4m
9	Turkey £65.7m
1	US £213.9m

2 | Who does Britain sell arms to?

● In 2004, the UK sold arms to 87 countries ... including Algeria, Iraq and Indonisia

| 6 | South Africa £86.5m |

Licensed UK Arms Exports 2004
Value of goods

3	Saudi Arabia £97.5m
4	Oman £91.9m
7	India £83.71m

● The UK's aid to sub-Saharan Africa is about one 40th of what it spends on defence

● Each year about half a million people are killed globally by armed violence

✳ The UN defines a "major war" as a military conflict leading to 1,000 battlefield deaths per year.

5 | Defence spending vs aid?

G7: Official development aid vs Defence expenditure 2003 Share of total government spending

USA   Defence spending 25%   Aid 1%

UK   Defence spending 13.3%   Aid 1.6%

6 | Who pays the price?

Civilian deaths

First World war

5%

Today

75%

How many major wars are being fought? ✳

1965

=10

2003

=15

STUDENT DESTINATIONS BROCHURE
Design by boing!

Client: De Montfort University Lincoln,
School of Applied Arts & Design
Design firm: boing!
Art direction: Jeff Leak and
Giles Woodward
Typography: Jeff Leak
Photography: Jeff Leak

This brochure had to present data concerning where graduates from De Montfort University in Lincoln, England, found employment. "We wanted the charts to convey something about the specific creative discipline they refer to," says Jeff Leak.

Each pie chart is created from a cut-out image of an item, or section of an item, that is directly associated with an individual academic discipline. For example, a piece of cut glass forms the pie chart for the BA Conservation and Restoration data, while a roll of masking tape forms the chart for the Foundation Studies diploma. The brochure is printed in two colors, with each pie chart shown in grayscale.

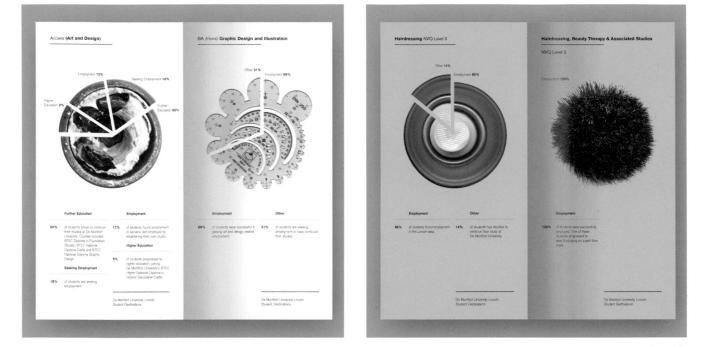

Access (Art and Design)

Employment **13%**
Seeking Employment **18%**
Higher Education **9%**
Further Education **60%**

Further Education

60% of students chose to continue their studies at De Montfort University. Courses included: BTEC Diploma in Foundation Studies, BTEC National Diploma Crafts and BTEC National Diploma Graphic Design.

Seeking Employment

18% of students are seeking employment.

Employment

13% of students found employment or became self-employed by establishing their own studio.

Higher Education

9% of students progressed to higher education, joining De Montfort University's BTEC Higher National Diploma in Historic Decorative Crafts.

De Montfort University Lincoln
Student Destinations

BA (Hons) Graphic Design and Illustration

Other **31%**
Employment **69%**

Employment

69% of students were successful in gaining art and design related employment.

Other

31% of students are seeking employment or have continued their studies.

De Montfort University Lincoln
Student Destinations

Hairdressing NVQ Level 3

Other **14%**
Employment **86%**

Employment

86% of students found employment in the Lincoln area.

Other

14% of students had decided to continue their study at De Montfort University.

De Montfort University Lincoln
Student Destinations

Hairdressing, Beauty Therapy & Associated Studies

NVQ Level 2

Employment **100%**

Employment

100% of students were successfully employed. One of these students progressed to level 3 studying on a part time basis.

De Montfort University Lincoln
Student Destinations

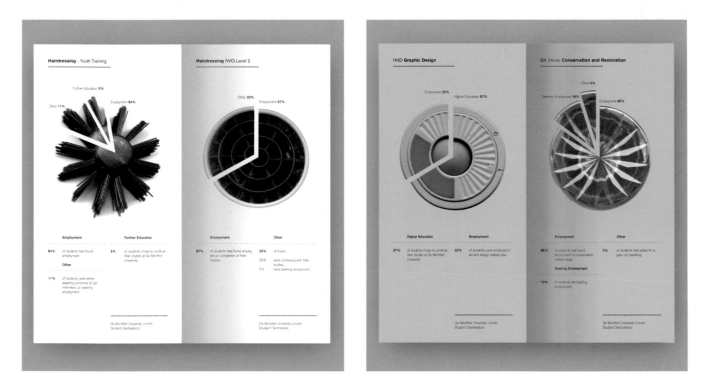

Hairdressing - Youth Training

Further Education **5%**
Other **11%**
Employment **84%**

Employment

84% of students had found employment.

Other

11% of students were either awaiting outcomes of job interviews, or seeking employment.

Further Education

5% of students chose to continue their studies at De Montfort University.

De Montfort University Lincoln
Student Destinations

Hairdressing NVQ Level 2

Other **33%**
Employment **67%**

Employment

67% of students had found employment on completion of their studies.

Other

33% of these;

28% were continuing with their studies.
5% were seeking employment.

De Montfort University Lincoln
Student Destinations

HND Graphic Design

Employment **33%**
Higher Education **67%**

Higher Education

67% of students chose to continue their studies at De Montfort University.

Employment

33% of students employed in art and design related jobs.

De Montfort University Lincoln
Student Destinations

BA (Hons) Conservation and Restoration

Other **5%**
Seeking Employment **10%**
Employment **85%**

Employment

85% of students had found employment in conservation related areas.

Seeking Employment

10% of students are seeking employment.

Other

5% of students had opted for a year out travelling.

De Montfort University Lincoln
Student Destinations

SEX SURVEY RESULTS
Design by Peter Grundy

Client: *Maxim* magazine New York
Design firm: Grundini Ltd.
Typography: Peter Grundy
Illustration: Peter Grundy

In written form, the results of this survey are unlikely to achieve the same impact as that achieved by Grundy's colorful and amusing interpretations. Charts are formed from simple images and text, with subtle typography used to clarify precise statistical facts. Throughout the piece, each mini diagram conveys complex statistical information in a simple, yet detailed manner. As with other examples of Peter Grundy's work, the reader is being invited to view this diagram from two different levels: the macro and the micro. The macro level promises the reader a humorous overview, whereas the micro level delivers detail.

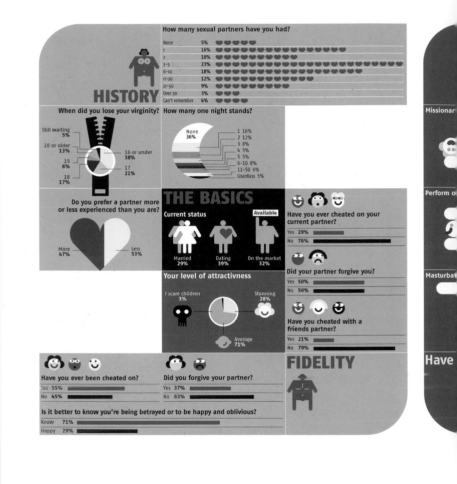

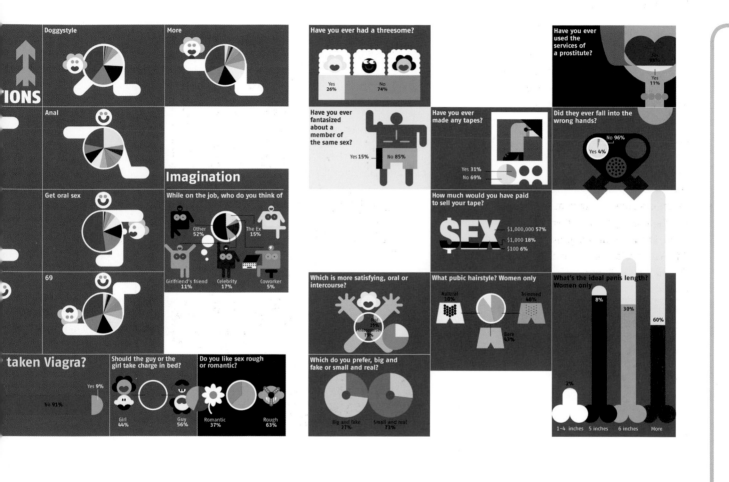

Doggystyle

More

Anal

Get oral sex

69

Imagination

While on the job, who do you think of

Other 52%
The Ex 15%
Girlfriend's friend 11%
Celebrity 17%
Coworker 5%

TIONS

taken Viagra?

Yes 9%
No 91%

Should the guy or the girl take charge in bed?
Girl 44%
Guy 56%

Do you like sex rough or romantic?
Romantic 37%
Rough 63%

Have you ever had a threesome?
Yes 26%
No 74%

Have you ever fantasized about a member of the same sex?
Yes 15%
No 85%

Which is more satisfying, oral or intercourse?
Oral 25%
Intercourse 75%

Which do you prefer, big and fake or small and real?
Big and fake 27%
Small and real 73%

Have you ever made any tapes?
Yes 31%
No 69%

How much would you have paid to sell your tape?
$EX
$1,000,000 57%
$1,000 18%
$100 6%

What pubic hairstyle? Women only
Natural 10%
Trimmed 46%
Bare 43%

Have you ever used the services of a prostitute?
No 89%
Yes 11%

Did they ever fall into the wrong hands?
No 96%
Yes 4%

What's the ideal penis length? Women only
2%
8%
30%
60%
1-4 inches
5 inches
6 inches
More

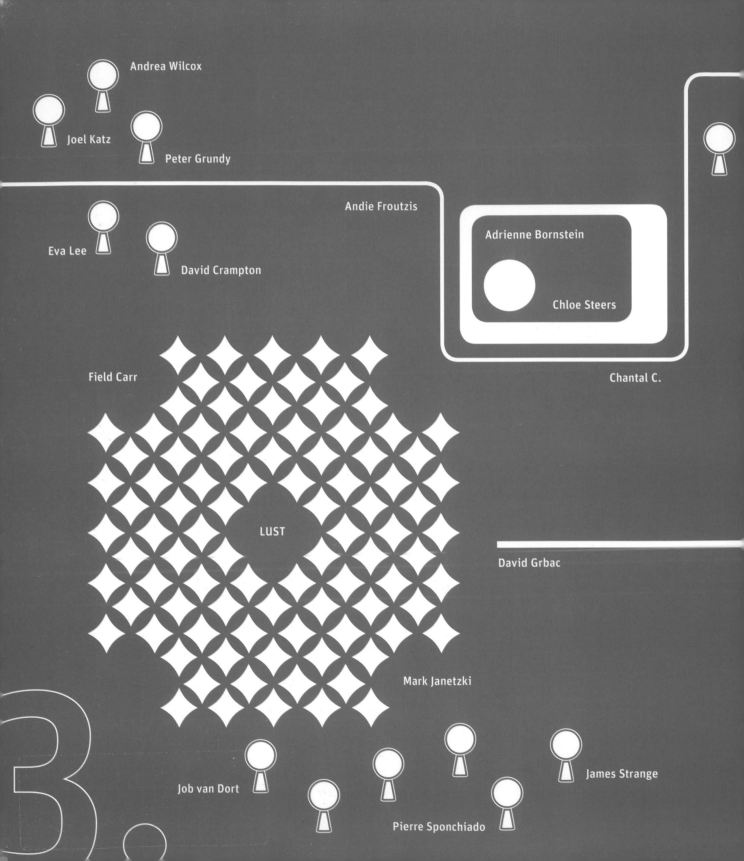

Environmental Design

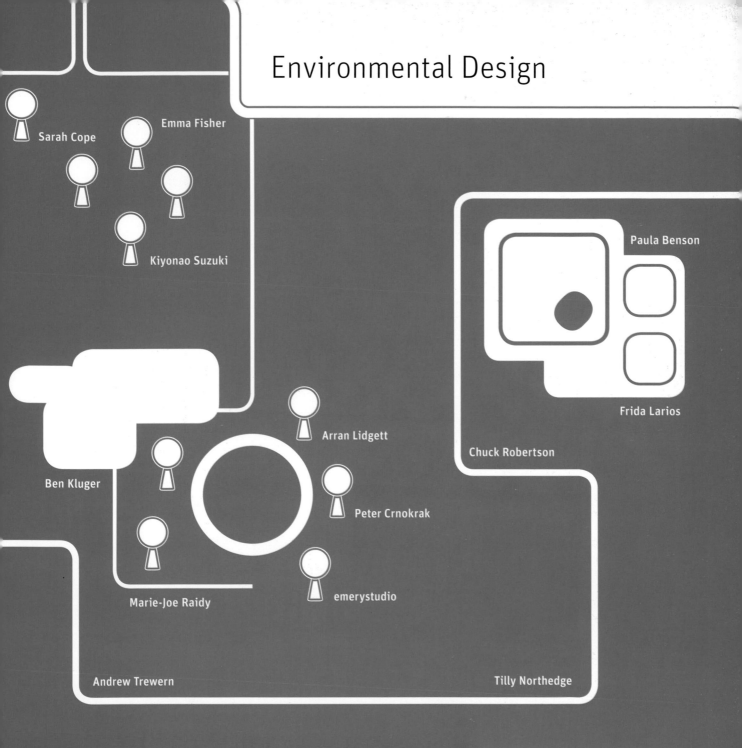

Sarah Cope

Emma Fisher

Kiyonao Suzuki

Paula Benson

Frida Larios

Chuck Robertson

Ben Kluger

Arran Lidgett

Peter Crnokrak

Marie-Joe Raidy

emerystudio

Andrew Trewern

Tilly Northedge

LEGACY NOW
Design by David Grbac

Client: EDAW
Design firm: Thomas Matthews
Art direction: Mark Beever
Photography: Amy Scaife
Project management: Clare Rohrsheim

Each interactive, publicly created diagram is reliant on the selection, grouping, and positioning of symbols; the ultimate aim of each game is to allow the public an easy method of communicating their own ambitions for the area to Olympic planners. Mark Beever's intention was to "create clear iconographic playing pieces that enable individuals to enjoy exploring the different possibilities for the development of their communities in an engaging manner."

Legacy Now is a public consultation concerning the layout, facilities, and ultimate legacy of the 2012 Olympic site in east London. Thomas Matthews designed an interactive board game based on colorful icons that can be distributed around a map of the site: the game is to be played in the open air by teams of six members of the public, each of whom is asked to give a helping hand in the planning of amenities such as housing, industry, social spaces, and cultural areas.

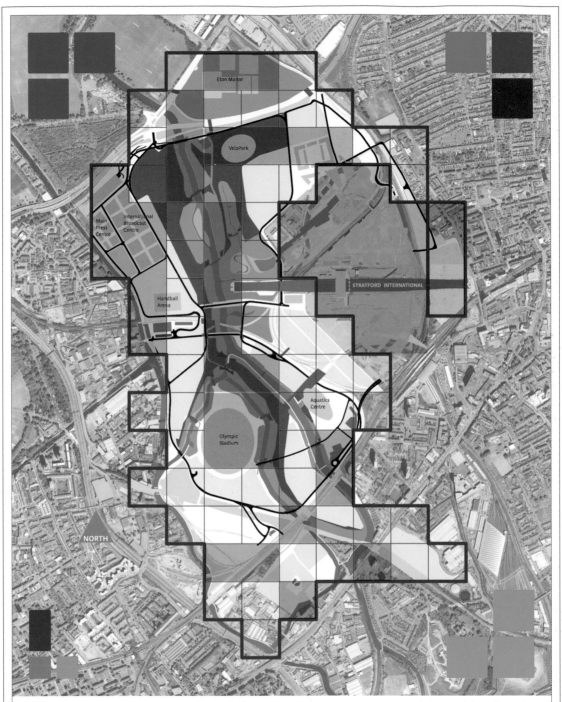

How to play

How would you plan to build the legacy of the Olympic Park? Use the playing pieces to create your own vision for the Park.

Choose your pieces carefully, you can only use the number of large squares which fit inside the red boundary.

Ask lots of questions to your friendly facilitator, they are here to help you plan, and to challenge your choices!

The playing pieces

Character areas

Key interest areas

Temporary venues

Community areas

Wildcard

Win a V.I.P visit to the Park

Enter your name on the card given to you by your facilitator at the end of your game to be entered to win a V.I.P visit to the Olympic Park early next year.

To enter, post your card in the slot below.

Icons were developed to symbolize three different kinds of housing: apartment blocks providing 3,000 homes, developments to provide another 500 homes, and smaller sites catering for 150 dwellings. Other symbols were created to communicate the desire for retail spaces, industrial spaces, and offices; and to represent health care, play, and sports facilities, wildlife areas, and schools. All of the symbols are clear and easy to understand, and slot simply over the proposed plan of the Olympic site.

The playing pieces

150 Homes	500 Homes	1000 Homes	20 Industry spaces	120 Office spaces	30 Retail stores	Public space

Character areas

Wildlife	Arts & culture	Cafes	Play areas	Active recreation	Allotments

Key interest areas

Hockey	Basketball	Fencing	BMX

Temporary venues

Schools	Healthcare	Community centre	Cycling	Local shops

Community areas

Wildcard

Wildcard

SPACE FOR ART/THE BIG SINK
Design by Chloe Steers

Client: The Clore Duffield Foundation
Design firm: SteersMcGillan Design Ltd.
Art direction: Richard McGillan
Illustration: Mike Cannings

It isn't often that diagrams use commissioned photography. This diagrammatic design by SteersMcGillan mixes black-and-white and full-color photography of hands to show the benefits of using high-quality architectural design within educational spaces. The hands, cut out from fingertip to wrist, are used in two ways. The diagram for section 01, which discusses the development process, uses six hands, proportionally scaled, to indicate the role played by different groups in the development of a learning space. The most significant influence clearly comes from the architects and financial backers of the project, with teachers and pupils playing a minor role. The section 08 diagram, concerning fittings, furniture, and equipment, uses full-color hands. A thumbs-up indicates that an item is essential, and a thumbs-down that equipment is not needed, while a hand signing the letter "O" identifies what is ideal.

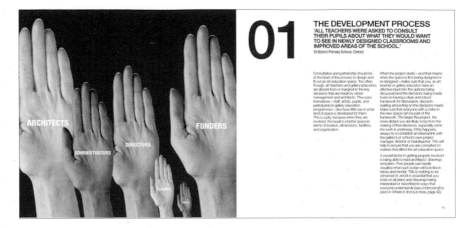

01

THE DEVELOPMENT PROCESS
'ALL TEACHERS WERE ASKED TO CONSULT THEIR PUPILS ABOUT WHAT THEY WOULD WANT TO SEE IN NEWLY DESIGNED CLASSROOMS AND IMPROVED AREAS OF THE SCHOOL.'
St Ebbe's Primary School, Oxford

08

FITTINGS, FURNITURE AND EQUIPMENT
'A PEGS LINE NEAR THE CEILING, A CUPBOARD FOR APRONS AND SAFE ART WORK THAT WE'RE NOT GOING TO PUT AROUND THE SCHOOL ... AND A BOARD FOR PUTTING YOUR WORK ON ... SHELVES WITH BOOKS ABOUT ART ... A MOSAIC FLOOR.'
Pupils from Lightwoods Community School, Oldbury

ESSENTIAL   IDEAL   NOT NEEDED

Please tick as appropriate

reference

The inspiration behind these images is the use of photomontage by fine artists such as Raoul Hausmann, cofounder of the Dada movement in Berlin.

SIGNAGE FOR THE 2007 LYON FESTIVAL OF LIGHTS
Design by Adrienne Bornstein and Pierre Sponchiado

Client: The city of Lyon
Design firm: Bornstein & Sponchiado
Photography: Adrienne Bornstein and
    Pierre Sponchiado

These diagrams are luminous displays. Their purpose is to inform the public about the work of an artist, together with sponsor details. Each artist is represented in a life-size photograph, from both the front and the back. Their photos are set next to, and within, a variety of measuring scales that indicate height, visual acuity, time and date of photograph, and the exact location of their work within the city of Lyon, France.

The topic of the festival—light—provided the inspiration for this work. Following this, Bornstein & Sponchiado sought to emulate the transparent properties of medical X-rays. "The X-ray codes are reproduced, amplified, and copied in order to maintain the illusion in the public's eye. Giving each image a front and a back entices people to roam around each luminous totem," says Adrienne Bornstein.

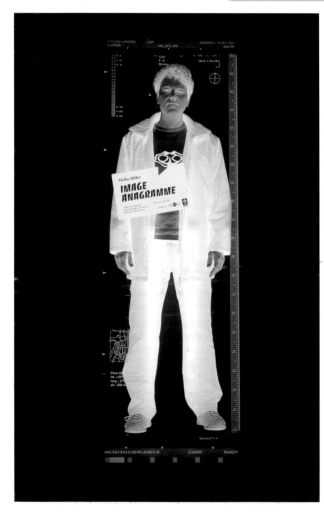

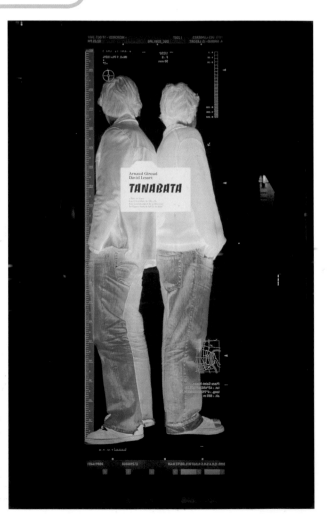

NEW YORK SUBWAY DEVELOPMENT DIAGRAM
Design by Peter Grundy

Client: Carl De Torres, Art Director
at Wired magazine USA
Design firm: Grundini Ltd.
Typography: Peter Grundy
Illustration: Peter Grundy

This diagram shows how a new subway is to be built, 15.25m (50ft) under the sidewalks of New York. Although, at first glance, the diagram appears very simple, much complex detail is presented. An amusing pile of bright-yellow cars is used to show the reader how deep the new subway will be, in a manner that is easy to comprehend. Figures of workmen are used to convey the height of the tunnel, and also the scale of the tunneling machines.

reference

Simplicity is a recurring theme in Grundy's work; cars, figures, and trees, along with many other details, are shown to great effect. Colors are used in a simple manner, as large areas of flat, childlike tone. Buildings feature many windows, but Grundy uses step-and-repeat carefully to ensure consistent positioning and repetition.

The route of the subway is shown, with Manhattan Island simplified to a near-rectangular shape, along with details of station stops and the main intersection at 72nd Street and Broadway.

Aboveground, skyscrapers, vehicles, machinery, and figures are used to give an idea of scale.

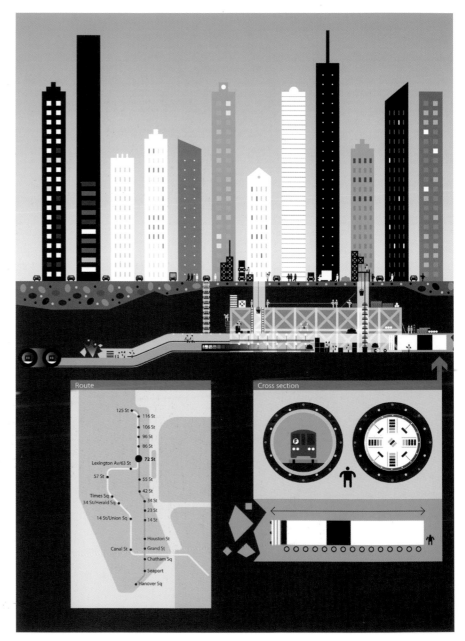

**RAIDY PRINTING GROUP
NEW PREMISES MAP
Design by Marie-Joe Raidy
and Chantal C.**

Client: Self-initiated
Design firm: Raidy Printing Group S.A.L.
Art direction: Marie-Joe Raidy
Illustration: Ziad AKL & Partners

reference

The diagrams, obviously inspired by the rollers of a printing press, show circular structural pillars, enveloped by curved, colorful walls that mimic the flow of paper through the rollers of the press.

These diagrammatic artist's impressions visualize the Raidy Printing Group's new premises in Beirut. From the design of the building, the onlooker can tell that Raidy's primary occupation is color printing.

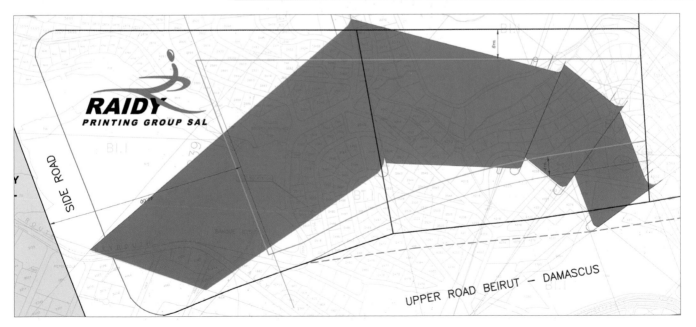

ZANDSTAD
Designed by LUST

Clients: The Netherlands Architecture
Fund, Rotterdam; and the Vrije
University, Amsterdam
Design firm: LUST

This project is a test case for working
within concepts of cultural biography
for an area, bringing together all
kinds of historical aspects, such as
architecture and landscape, religion
and occupations. The objective is for
designers and historians to work
together in developing concepts for
new developments. Zandstad is
a fictional region, set in the area
of Eindhoven in the Netherlands,
and in the process of restructuring,
developing from a mainly agricultural
to a more diversified area. Real regions
that share characteristics with the
fictional Zandstad, together with
the diagrams that accompany this
project, will be used to inform new
areas of development.

These diagrams are concerned with
the fact that maps are not always
truthful interpretations of factual detail.
A map can be an abstraction of reality,
with certain choices made due to
factors such as scale. The cartography
designed for Zandstad deliberately
"lies" by isolating data and plotting
this information in ways that force
a specific narrative. A good example
is the reordering of satellite photos of
the area based on land use, including
such categories as forestry, water,
agriculture, urban residential, and
rural residential.

Other project outcomes include
visualization of the impact of pig
farming on Zandstad. LUST designed
a series of animated flythrough
diagrams using individual red houses
to represent pig farms, and a dome to
represent the circle of smell that would
pervade the surrounding area. This
simple diagram makes a clear visual
case as to why residential development
would be restricted in this location.

**While LUST made no comment about
their inspiration for this piece, we think
the traditional Monopoly houses surely
influenced them in some way.**

GOLDSMITHS 09/10
UNDERGRADUATE PROSPECTUS
Design by Paula Benson and Arran Lidgett

Client: Goldsmiths, University of London
Design firm: Form
Art direction: Paula Benson
Illustration: Nathan Dytor
Photography: Bill Robinson, Ivan Coleman, and Geoff Wilson

Form designed three maps for the Goldsmiths 09/10 undergraduate prospectus; each successive map locates the viewer closer to the actual university campus. The first map shows Goldsmiths' location in relation to the greater London area; the second takes the reader in closer to New Cross, southeast London; and the final map shows campus buildings, tube stations, and road names. The project has a great clarity in design, taking the reader from the macro to the micro in a manner that is easy to understand.

Throughout each of the maps, roads are shown in dark gray with road names reversed out in white, focusing the viewer on these thoroughfares. Where more detail is shown, such as the local environment, muted tones are used in order to keep the focus on the important cartographic information.

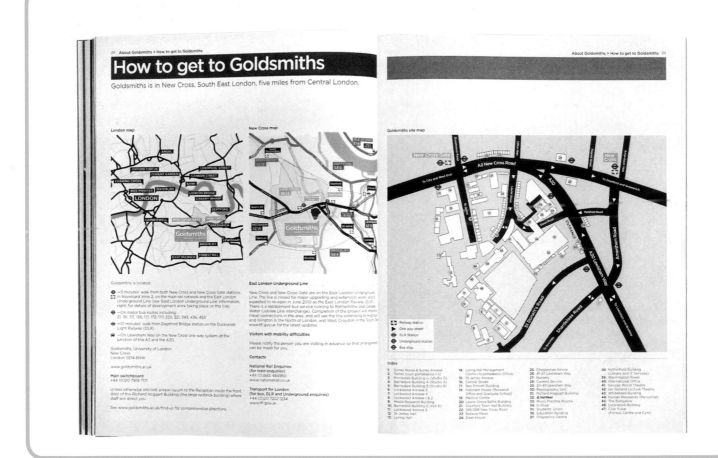

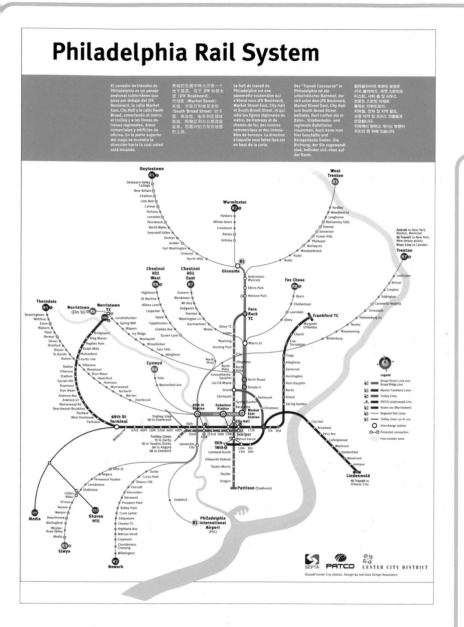

PHILADELPHIA RAIL SYSTEM MAP
Design by Joel Katz

Client: Self-initiated
Design firm: Joel Katz Design Associates
Art direction: Joel Katz
Typography: Joel Katz

Maps for rapid transport systems are, almost without exception, complex and detailed, and this is certainly true of metropolitan Philadelphia's trolley, rapid rail, and commuter rail system. This map includes detail concerned not only with connections, routes, and shared track, but also stations with disabled access. Joel Katz has applied design innovations to the mapping system in order to present this information in the clearest way. These innovations include the use of a radial rather than a 45° or 90° vocabulary, varying line thickness to denote individual or shared tracks, and an improved visual language to denote connections and free transfers. The map also features icons clearly identifying disabled access, and allows for the addition of multilingual explanations. A successful feature of many transport maps, each transportation route is also color-coded.

THE HAGUE UNDERGROUND
Design by LUST

Client: Stroom Den Haag
Design firm: LUST
Art direction: LUST

Stroom is a foundation for art, visual culture, and architecture in The Hague, the Netherlands. Its program for the Day of Architecture 2006 was centered around the city's rarely considered underground features. Many of these hidden sites were opened up for the day, with tours and excursions to explore these secret and forgotten places organized.

This map was designed as a guide for the tours and excursions, and also as a useful diagrammatic archive of The Hague's underground locations. It consists only of elements that are below ground: what initially appears to be a grid of streets is, in fact, a plan of the main parts of the sewerage system of the city.

Other elements included are underground parking areas, underground rivers, archeological sites, bunkers, and proposed future underground structures. Each element was printed in a different shade of black ink, and through the process of overprinting, a wide array of special shades of black was created. The areas highlighted, as though by spray painting against a mask or stencil, are the underground sites to be visited during the excursions.

reference

LUST's inspiration for this design clearly comes from the subtle and uncommon print possibilities that occur as a result of overprinting a range of different special black inks.

BLACK SUN MAP
Design by Peter Grundy

Client: Black Sun Design PLC
Design firm: Grundini Ltd.
Typography: Peter Grundy
Illustration: Peter Grundy

The aim of these maps by Peter Grundy is not simply to explain to the reader how to reach their ultimate destination, but also to give them an idea of what they will see during their journey.

The macro view provides the contextual information, with details including road names and public transport links. The micro view zooms in on specific features, promising an expanse of green space, gardens, and mature trees.

These captivating designs use bold flat color and simple shapes that are, for the most part, reduced to rectangles, circles, and heavy rules. In Peter Grundy's delightful world, rows of vehicles are parked equidistantly in straight lines; each car is identical to the others and all point in the same direction. A similar, pleasing repetition is applied to trees. Subliminally, this use of repetition helps to reassure the viewer that this will be an easy map to follow, and therefore, a simple and enjoyable journey to make.

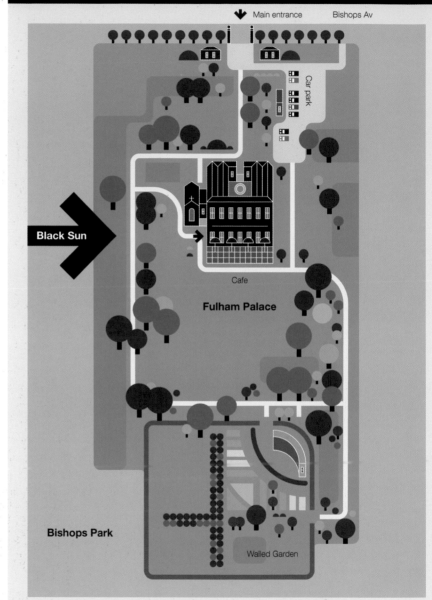

Finding Black Sun at Fulham Palace

Main entrance   Bishops Av

Car park

Black Sun

Cafe

Fulham Palace

Bishops Park

Walled Garden

Black Sun plc The Fulham Palace Bishops Avenue London SW6 6EA Telephone +44 (0)20 7736 0011

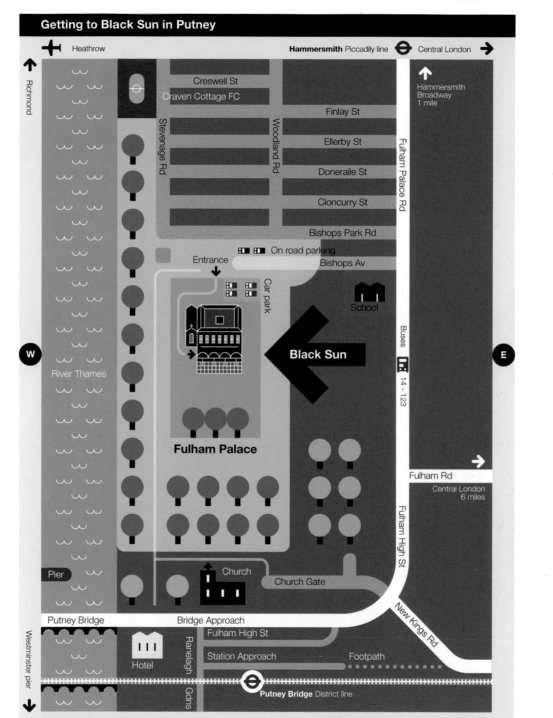

Getting to Black Sun in Putney

✈ Heathrow

Hammersmith Piccadily line ● Central London →

Richmond

Heathrow

Creswell St
Craven Cottage FC

Stevenage Rd

Woodland Rd

Finlay St

Ellerby St

Doneraile St

Cloncurry St

Bishops Park Rd

On road parking

Entrance

Bishops Av

Car park

Hammersmith
Broadway
1 mile

Fulham Palace Rd

School

W

Black Sun

E

Buses

14 - 123

River Thames

Fulham Rd

Central London
6 miles

Fulham Palace

Fulham High St

Pier

Church

Church Gate

New Kings Rd

Putney Bridge

Bridge Approach

Fulham High St

Westminster pier

Hotel

Ranelagh Gdns

Station Approach

Footpath

● **Putney Bridge** District line

Black Sun plc The Fulham Palace Bishops Avenue London SW6 6EA Telephone +44 (0)20 7736 0011

NEW MAYA LANGUAGE WAYFINDING SYSTEM
Design by Frida Larios

Client: Self-initiated
Art direction: Frida Larios
Typography: Frida Larios

The information being communicated in these diagrams and maps relates to the Maya, who lived in the Mesoamerican region (Central America) from 1500 BC to AD 1519. Mesoamerica is one of the world's six cradles of civilization, though their intelligent and beautifully written language is unknown to the Western world. The position of scribe in Mayan society was a very privileged one. Not only were scribes artists, sculptors, and calligraphers, they were also astronomers, mathematicians, historians, and bookkeepers.

As part of her research for the project, Larios investigated how the Maya scriptures could be adapted for contemporary use. The result of her research is a graphic system that she has named New Maya Language. It involves a redesign of certain Mayan ideographs that communicate concepts and even sentences. Larios' diagrams explain how these symbols can be interpreted and combined, for example, by bringing the words stone and fire together to mean "lava stone."

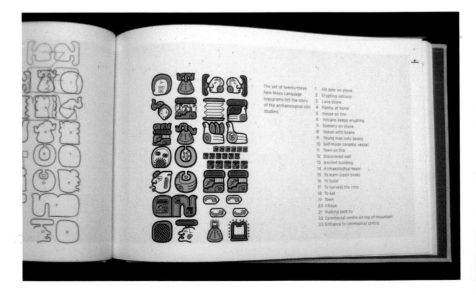

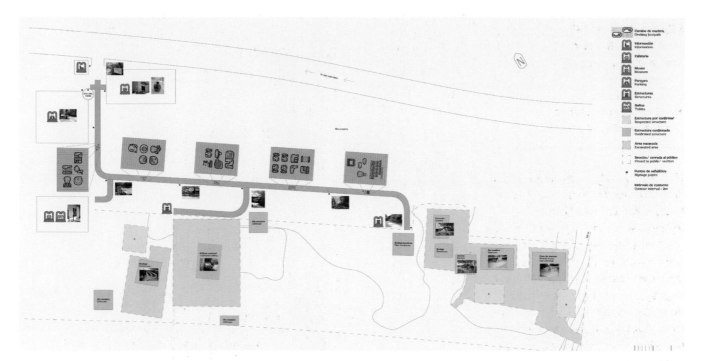

This map is for Joya de Cerén, a UNESCO World Heritage Site in El Salvador. It mixes New Maya Language pictograms with color photography to communicate the story of this historic site to visitors.

"As a central American living away from home for six years, I was inspired to research, and attempt to resuscitate, the unique Maya scriptures, which have been undervalued by local graphic designers and could be reformed for application in contemporary visual communications," explains Larios.

GREEN PARK MAP
Design by Peter Grundy

Client: Brownjohn Ltd.
Design firm: Grundini Ltd.
Typography: Peter Grundy
Illustration: Peter Grundy

This Green Park map is packed with information; not just a route finder, it also shows, in tremendous detail, the buildings, landscaping, parking, and power sources of the area.

The use of perspective allows such fine detail that the number of windows and floors in each building can be accurately represented. Buildings are color-coded to distinguish incomplete or planned properties from their completed neighbors. Interestingly, the reader is given a completely different view of the surrounding landscape; for this Grundy presents a bird's-eye view.

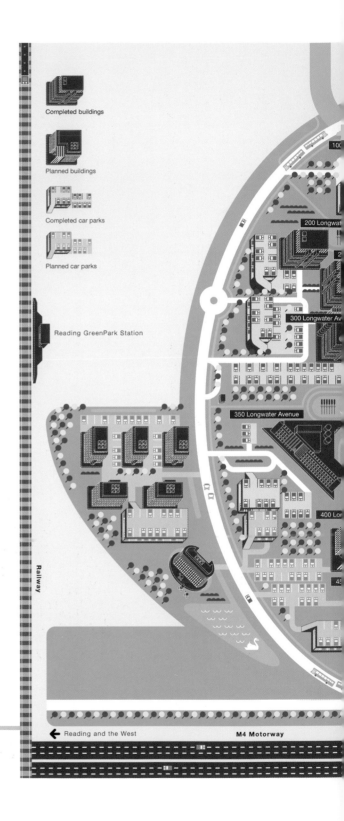

Completed buildings

Planned buildings

Completed car parks

Planned car parks

Reading GreenPark Station

100

200 Longwat

300 Longwater Av

350 Longwater Avenue

400 Lor

45

Railway

← Reading and the West

M4 Motorway

Longwater Avenue

Brook Drive

100 Brook Drive

200 Brook Drive

250 Brook Drive

300 Brook Drive

350 Brook Drive

400 Brook Drive

450 Brook Drive

500 Brook Drive

Reading Gate Retail Park

The Millennium Madejski Hotel

Madejski Stadium and Conference Centre

A33

Costco

250 South Oak Way

Lime Sq

Cannons Health Club

lsq2 Bar

Nursery

280 South Oak Way

260 South Oak Way

400 South Oak Way

South Oak Way

Wind Turbine and Visitor Centre

500 South Oak Way

450 South Oak Way

300 South Oak Way

London and the East →

NEOPOLIS MASTER PLAN
Design by Peter Crnokrak

Client: NeoPolis
Design firm: the apartment with
Alberto Foyo Architects
Art direction: Stefan Boublil
Illustration: Peter Crnokrak

NeoPolis is a conceptual visualization
of the development of a technology
park in the Ukraine. The NeoPolis Master
Plan is the first of seven master-plan
brochures that fold out into posters
to reveal each phase of the park's
development. It shows the percentage
of land use per development phase
using proportionately scaled black dots.
This allows for relatively small differences
in land use to be assessed, and as such
helps to make the case for the actual
construction of the master plan as shown.

NeoPolis is a conceptual visualization of the development of a techno-park in the Ukraine. Particular care was taken to envision a mixed-use, phased development that was ecologically sensitive and sustainable. The NeoPolis master plan contained in this document was created by New York design agency, the apartment.

OFFICE COMPONENT / КОМПОНЕНТ ОФИСА

GREEN BOULEVARD / ЗЕЛЕНЫЙ БУЛЬВАР

KIEV ROAD & GREEN ARTERY / ДОРОГА КИЕВ & ЗЕЛЕНАЯ АРТЕРИЯ

RESIDENTIAL COMPONENT / ЖИЛОЙ КОМПЛЕКС

Site Area 0.5² km
Зона места 0.5² km

THAMES GATEWAY DIAGRAM/MAP
**Design by Peter Grundy
and Tilly Northedge**

Client: CABE (Commission for
    Architecture and the
    Built Environment)
Design firm: Grundini Ltd.
Art direction: Peter Grundy
Typography: Peter Grundy
Illustration: Peter Grundy and
    Tilly Northedge

This commission visualizes the complex development plans for the Thames Gateway area in London. Grundy's aim was to produce a map/diagram that functions well as a poster or a leaflet in order to make the complex not only simple, but also portable. The map shows an intricate network of road and rail links set at angles of 45° or 90°. The urban areas are shaded pale yellow, with less populated and costal locations shaded white and gray. In this "world" the river Thames and its tributaries flow along a horizontal route, with the occasional change of direction to 45°. The shape of the coastal area has also been simplified to follow the same horizontal, vertical, and 45° alignment. Rounded corners and repetition are striking elements here. Simplified icons are used to great effect, with lollipop-shaped trees denoting parkland and woodland, and a bird in flight indicating areas rich in biodiversity. The yellow panel across the bottom of the map holds additional information about the region. The images and icons here follow the same design approach as that used for the map itself, thus ensuring cohesion throughout the design.

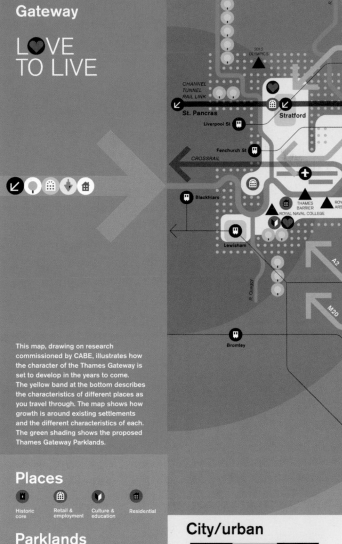

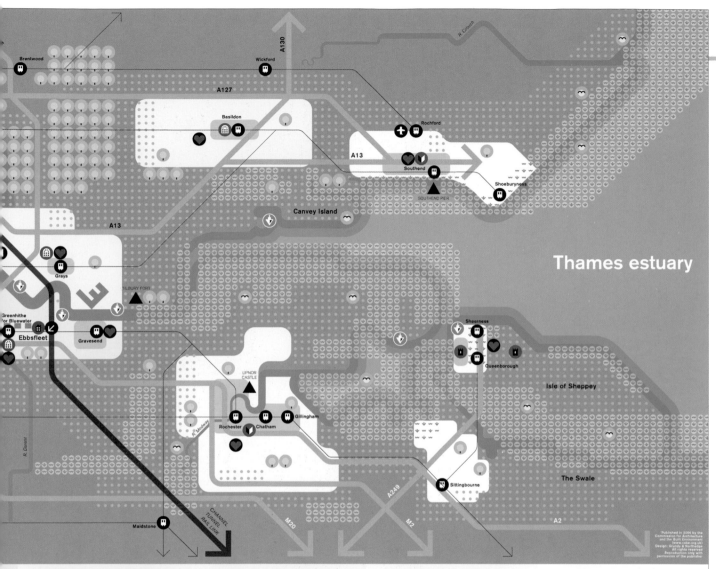

Brentwood

Wickford

A130

A127

Basildon

Rochford

A13

Southend

Shoeburyness

SOUTHEND PIER

Canvey Island

Thames estuary

A13

Grays

TILBURY FORT

Greenhithe
for Bluewater

Ebbsfleet

Gravesend

R. Darent

Sheerness

Queenborough

Isle of Sheppey

UPNOR
CASTLE

R. Medway

Rochester Chatham Gillingham

The Swale

CHANNEL
TUNNEL
RAIL LINK

Maidstone

M20

A249

M2

Sittingbourne

A2

Industry/country

High-density mixed-use urban regeneration
focused on existing urban settlements, as
seen here north of the river. Large-scale
industrial and retail development

150-200/ha

Country/urban

Mixed-use, medium-density urban
extensions, such as around Basildon.
Close proximity to natural open spaces

100-150/ha

Country/estuary

Medium to high-density mixed-use infill
developments enhancing existing historic
settlements in close proximity to estuary
and country parks

150-200/ha

Estuary/sea

Sensitive renewal of existing towns and
villages with a close relationship to the
estuary landscape.

50-100/ha

VICTORIA UNIVERSITY MAP
Design by emerystudio

Client: Victoria University
Design firm: emerystudio
Art direction: Garry Emery

emerystudio produced two diagrams as part of this project for Victoria University, Australia. The first provides a micro view of the university's Werribee Campus, and the second, an associated map, locates the campus within the complex local road network.

Solid blue shapes with rounded corners are used to represent rooms and corridors, with entrances clearly indicated for every location. Unlike many floor plans, this design has no drawn walls or divisional barriers—these elements are indicated simply by leaving equidistant spaces between interconnecting locations. As a result, the design gives the impression that the campus is one large, fluid shape.

The accompanying map provides the reader with a macro view of Victoria University, with areas of buildings indicated more generally using the now-familiar blue shapes with rounded corners.

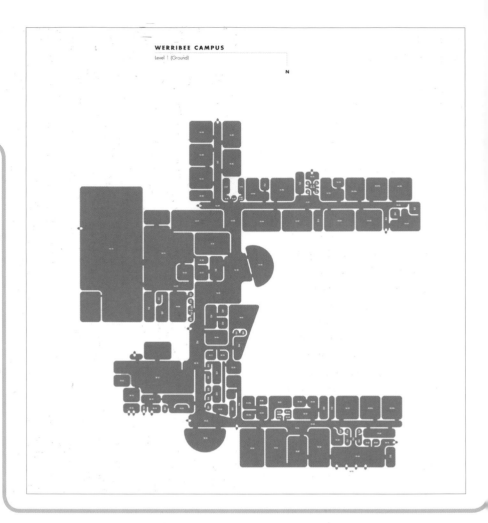

WERRIBEE CAMPUS
Level 1 (Ground)

TAIPEI 101
Design by emerystudio

Client: Taipei 101
Design firm: emerystudio
Art direction: Garry Emery

Taipei 101 is the name given to the world's tallest building, towering 509m (1,670ft) above ground, in Taiwan. It also has a number of levels underground. This plan of some of the public spaces within the building details the layout and amenities on just one floor; it also shows the underground levels and color-coded parking zones. From the diagram, the viewer can see that the tower itself is divided into eight tapered sections—eight is considered a lucky number in China, and this element was deliberately incorporated in the structure.

reference

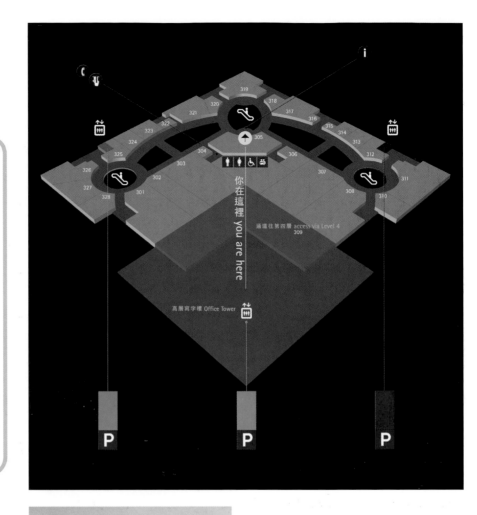

MELBOURNE MUSEUM FLOOR PLAN
Design by emerystudio

Client: Melbourne Museum
Design firm: emerystudio
Art direction: Garry Emery

Melbourne Museum explores life in the Australian state of Victoria, from its natural environment to its culture and heritage. The award-winning museum houses a permanent collection in eight galleries, including one specifically for children. The outside of the building features a vivid square of bright color samples, and emerystudio used these shades on the plan to indicate the different areas in the exhibition space. The colors take on an even brighter appearance in the plan, as they are set against a black background for maximum contrast.

reference

The memorable architecture of the Melbourne Museum, in Victoria, Australia, is the clear inspiration behind the visitor's map produced by emerystudio.

You are on **Ground level**

Children's Museum
Big Box
Tattersall's Children's Garden
Science and Life Gallery
Evolution Gallery
Forest Gallery
Bunjilaka
Milarri Garden
Te Pasifika Gallery
Schools Entrance
Activity Rooms
Paddle Pop Playground
Museum Shop
Brasserie
Tuckshop

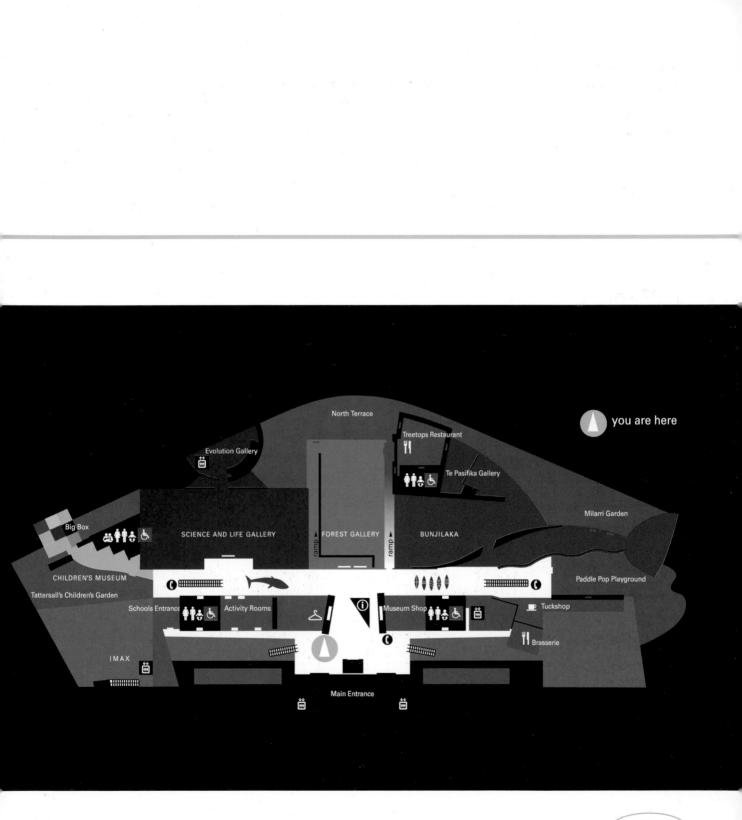

you are here

North Terrace

Treetops Restaurant

Evolution Gallery

Te Pasifika Gallery

Milarri Garden

Big Box

SCIENCE AND LIFE GALLERY

FOREST GALLERY

BUNJILAKA

Paddle Pop Playground

CHILDREN'S MUSEUM

Tattersall's Children's Garden

Tuckshop

Schools Entrance

Activity Rooms

Museum Shop

Brasserie

IMAX

Main Entrance

THE IAN POTTER CENTRE: FLOOR PLAN
Design by Andrew Trewern, Ben Kluger, David Crampton, Job van Dort, Sarah Cope, Eva Lee, Emma Fisher, Andie Froutzis, and Andrea Wilcox

Client: The Ian Potter Centre,
    National Gallery of Victoria
Design firm: emerystudio
Art direction: Garry Emery

This design uses various shades of gray to distinguish between exhibition spaces, amenities, and foyer areas. Gray was selected to echo the tones of the building itself. Each of the three plans uses a selection of simple, brightly colored icons to point the visitor in the direction of stairs, elevators, restrooms, information desks, and other essential conveniences. The center houses over 20 galleries featuring an impressive selection of Australian art, and each display space has been given a code number that is set in a distinctive contemporary typeface.

G19 temporary exhibitions

G18 temporary exhibitions

G20 temporary exhibitions

G17 temporary exhibitions

crossbar café

G16 temporary exhibitions

G13 temporary exhibitions

G15 temporary exhibitions

G14 temporary exhibitions

LEVEL 3
temporary exhibitions G13–G20
photography
prints and drawings
fashion and textiles

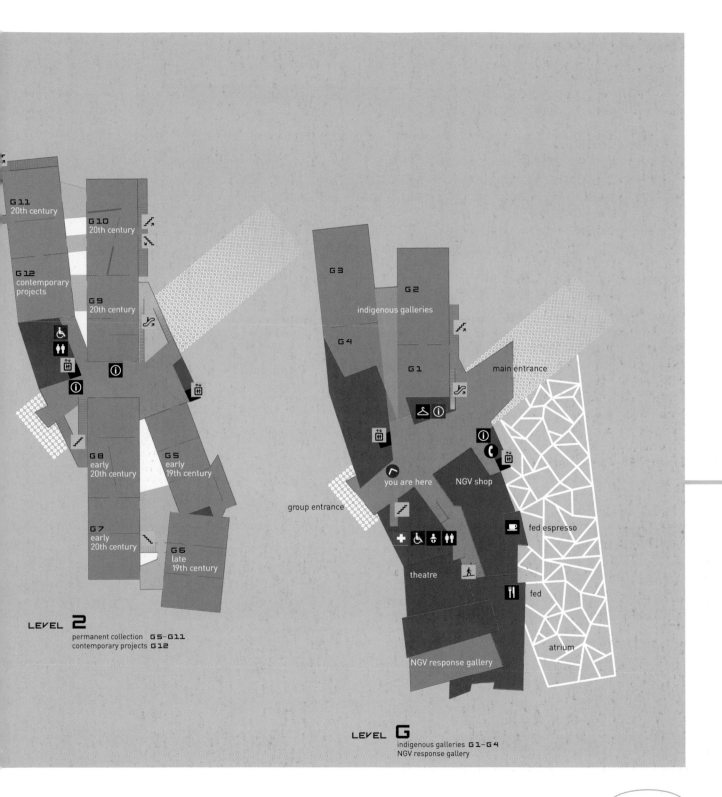

G11
20th century

G10
20th century

G12
contemporary
projects

G9
20th century

G8
early
20th century

G5
early
19th century

G7
early
20th century

G6
late
19th century

G3

G2

indigenous galleries

G4

G1

main entrance

you are here

NGV shop

group entrance

theatre

fed espresso

fed

atrium

NGV response gallery

LEVEL 2

permanent collection G5–G11
contemporary projects G12

LEVEL G

indigenous galleries G1–G4
NGV response gallery

PROVO TOWNE CENTRE
WAYFINDING SYSTEM
Design by James Strange

Client: Provo Towne Centre Shopping Mall
Design firm: Greteman Group
Art direction: Sonia Greteman

The Greteman Group was commissioned to design the wayfinding system for The Provo Towne Centre shopping mall, which includes retail outlets, a food court, a cinema, and a children's play area. The project included entry signage and locator maps, along with signage for the food court. The system uses bright colors—blue, red, and white—and backlighting to highlight detail and increase legibility.

reference

As Sonia Greteman explains, "Utah is known for its open spaces and big skies full of thousands of twinkling stars." The Greteman Group picked up on this notable characteristic to give an identity and sense of place to their design, incorporating stars on their decorative information panels, along with a "celestial" logo.

LIBERTY PARK CONSTRUCTION FENCE
Design by Chuck Robertson

Client: Brookfield Properties
Design firm: Doyle Partners
Art direction: Tom Kluepfel

Featuring a number of unverified statements, or factoids, along with factual information about new amenities and features of the area, the Liberty Park construction fence uses a highly colorful chart to inform the "passing public" about developments and, of course, to hide a construction site. The context for this vast, extremely noticeable piece of diagrammatic design is the busy downtown streets of Manhattan, full of urban clutter, people, traffic, and skyscrapers.

"The information within this chart is broken into 'fun-to-eat' pieces that pedestrians, and people in very slow taxis, can pick up and digest," says Rosemarie Turk of Doyle Partners. Each section of the chart features a motif made from circles, or sections of circles, with the number of circles carefully selected to communicate a particular fact or factoid.

The inspirations behind this design are the colorful worlds of pop and op art, and the flat opaque color of origami paper and the shades and shapes found in 1960s fabric patterns.

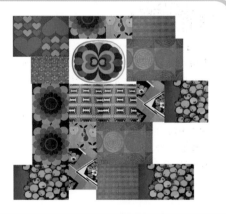

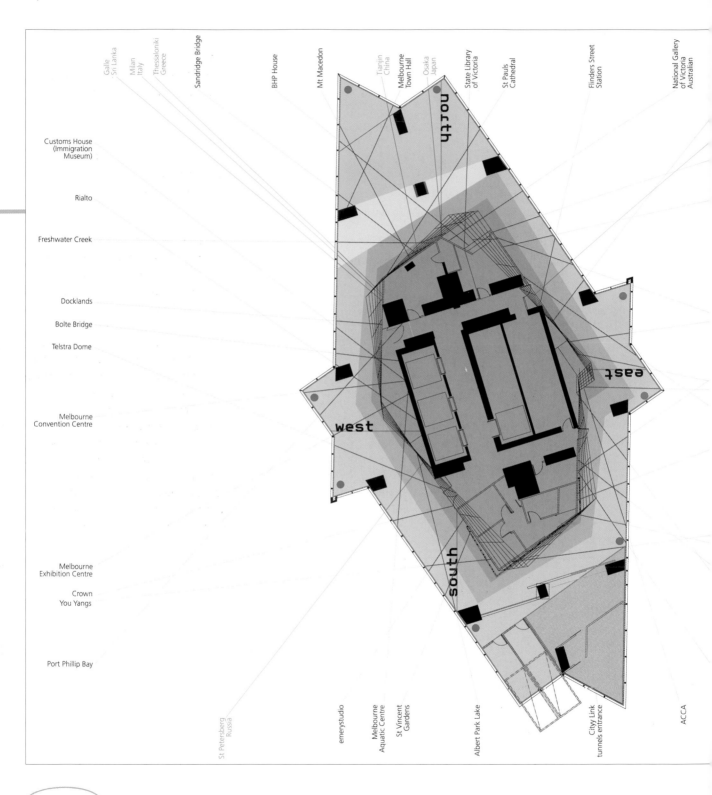

Galle
Sri Lanka

Milan
Italy

Thessaloniki
Greece

Sandridge Bridge

BHP House

Mt Macedon

Tianjin
China

Melbourne
Town Hall

Osaka
Japan

State Library
of Victoria

St Pauls
Cathedral

Flinders Street
Station

National Gallery
of Victoria
Australian

Customs House
(Immigration
Museum)

Rialto

Freshwater Creek

Docklands

Bolte Bridge

Telstra Dome

Melbourne
Convention Centre

Melbourne
Exhibition Centre

Crown
You Yangs

Port Phillip Bay

St Petersberg
Russia

emerystudio

Melbourne
Aquatic Centre

St Vincent
Gardens

Albert Park Lake

City Link
tunnels entrance

ACCA

north

west

east

south

DIAGRAMS: Innovative Solutions for Graphic Designers

Boston
USA

Birrarung Marr

Hamer Hall

Fitzroy Gardens

MCG

Victorian Arts Centre

Sidney Myer Music Bowl
Mt Dandenong

Olympic Park

Melbourne Park

Government House

National Gallery of Victoria International

———— view indicator and floor marker
———— infinity column (Barco)
● digital telescopes

0   1m   5m

N

Shrine of
Rememberance

Royal Botanic
Gardens

EUREKA SKYDECK
**Design by Mark Janetzki, Ben Kluger,
Field Carr, Job van Dort, and
Kiyonao Suzuki**

Client: Melbourne Eureka Tower
    Observation Deck Pty. Ltd.
Design firm: emerystudio
Art direction: Garry Emery

The Eureka Skydeck, in Melbourne,
Australia, is situated on the 88th floor
of the world's tallest residential building,
some 300m (985ft) above ground. This
floor plan shows, in cross section, the
surprising shape of the structure, complete
with its famous "glass box" that extends
3m (10ft) into open air. The plan not only
shows the internal divisions and structure
of the space, but also cleverly highlights
significant vantage points, from which
visitors can view locations of note within
the city of Melbourne and beyond. These
vantage points are linked with red lines
that join up and crisscross the floor
plan and extend beyond the walls of the
building, in light gray, to helpfully join
to the name of the location of note.

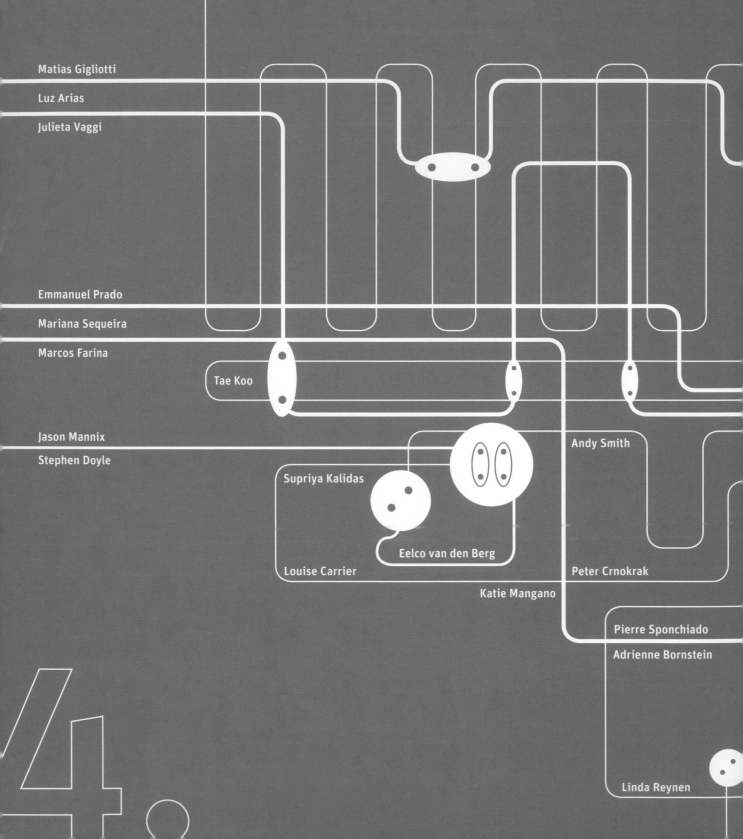

Matias Gigliotti

Luz Arias

Julieta Vaggi

Emmanuel Prado

Mariana Sequeira

Marcos Farina

Tae Koo

Jason Mannix

Stephen Doyle

Andy Smith

Supriya Kalidas

Eelco van den Berg

Louise Carrier

Katie Mangano

Peter Crnokrak

Pierre Sponchiado

Adrienne Bornstein

Linda Reynen

4.

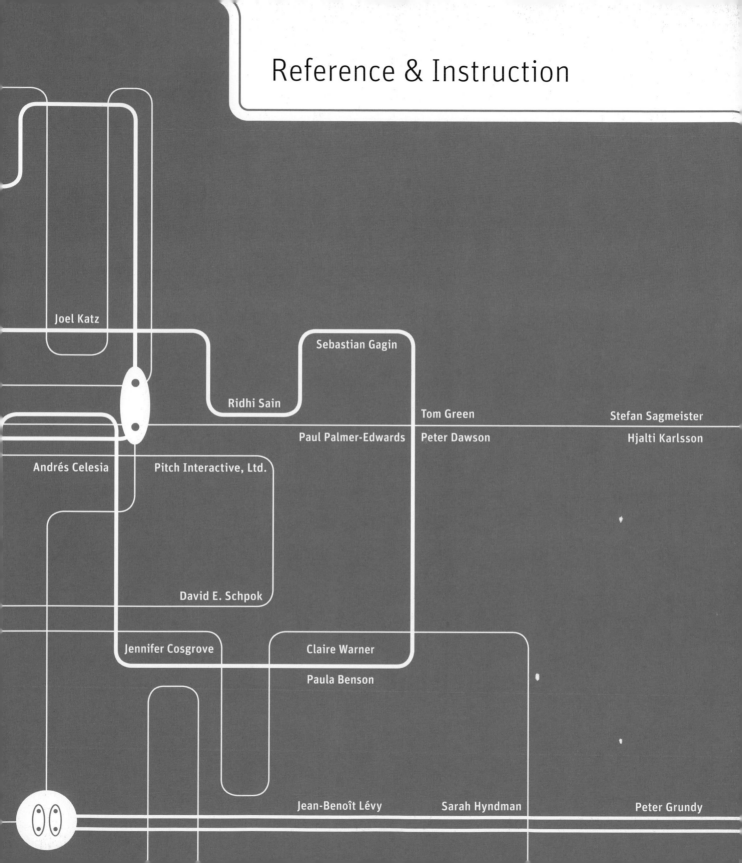

Reference & Instruction

Joel Katz

Sebastian Gagin

Ridhi Sain

Tom Green

Stefan Sagmeister

Paul Palmer-Edwards

Peter Dawson

Hjalti Karlsson

Andrés Celesia

Pitch Interactive, Ltd.

David E. Schpok

Jennifer Cosgrove

Claire Warner

Paula Benson

Jean-Benoît Lévy

Sarah Hyndman

Peter Grundy

STOCKHOLM NETWORK
ANNUAL REPORT
Design by Sarah Hyndman

Client: Stockholm Network
Design firm: With Relish
Art direction: Sarah Hyndman
Satellite image: http://visibleearth.
nasa.gov

The Stockholm Network annual report
uses diagrams to indicate different
areas of growth, expansion, and
information dissemination throughout
the year. A key objective of this project
is to speak to an international audience
without a shared first language. The aim
was to avoid the overuse of lists, tables,
and verbose descriptions that might
put readers off. Graphic visualizations
convey the company's increasing
global profile, using images of satellites
beaming down onto an expanded map
of the world. To speak specifically of
company growth, With Relish has used
a spider diagram composed of green
speech bubbles and yellow arrows set
against the image of a mature oak tree.

Inspiring Growth
The Stockholm Network Annual Report 2007/08

STOCKHOLM
NETWORK

The inspiration behind the Global Outreach designs was the wonderful images on NASA's Visible Earth website. This site offers an impressive range of photographs and diagrams that provide visual information concerning the planet Earth.

Global Outreach

As policy debates have become globalised, the value of our comparative approach now has an ever-wider appeal. The work of the Stockholm Network today reaches beyond the shores of the European continent. Our research projects and our network extend outwards; no longer exclusively within and between European countries – although this remains central to our mission – but also beyond their borders.

The Stockholm Network is now creating fresh dialogue and a new exchange of policy ideas between Europe and other parts of the globe, in both the developed and the developing world.

"The Stockholm Network, in addition to its extensive involvement in the European policy debate, is now increasing its coverage in the rest of the world, my Chile included. That is great news to all lovers of freedom."

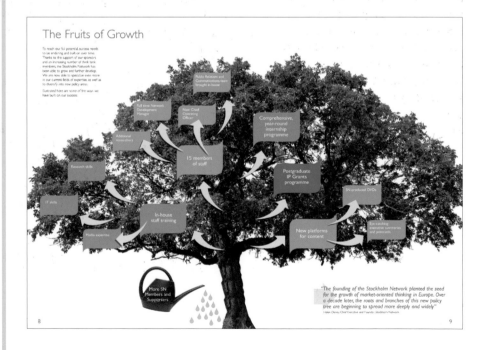

The Fruits of Growth

"The founding of the Stockholm Network planted the seed for the growth of market-oriented thinking in Europe. Over a decade later, the roots and branches of this new policy tree are beginning to spread more deeply and widely"

BODYPARTS DIAGRAM
Design by Peter Grundy

Client: *Esquire* magazine
Design firm: Grundini Ltd.
Typography: Peter Grundy
Illustration: Peter Grundy

"The idea behind this diagram is the fact that one of the most effective ways of informing an audience is to entertain them," says Peter Grundy of his design for *Esquire* magazine. In characteristic style, Grundy's design brings together simplified shapes, mainly with rounded corners, to create a fascinating and humorous anatomical diagram.

The stomach is a rectangle, the liver a triangle, and the spleen and kidney are variations on a heart shape. This stylized approach does not involve showing any of the possibly disturbing, realistic detail that may put off some *Esquire* readers—not a single scalpel cut or speck of blood is shown.

However, this piece does not only amuse, it also clearly and effectively communicates a serious message, namely the value, in pounds sterling, of each major organ.

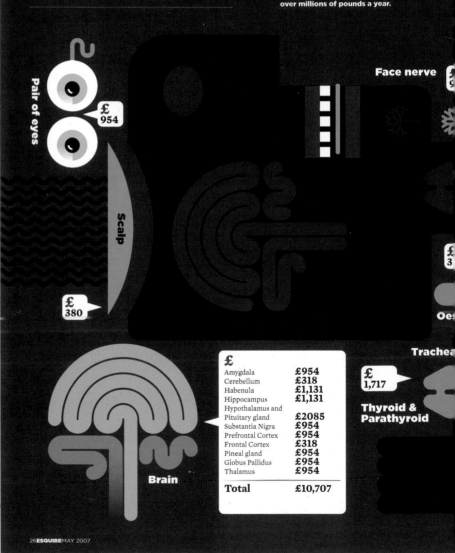

Inquirescience

Price on your head

How to turn a recently dead loved one into a Mercedes-Benz SLK

BODYSNATCHERS BURKE AND HARE MAY BE TURNING IN THEIR GRAVES, but at least they won't be snatched up from them. Today's scientists have rejected graverobbing in favour of 'human tissue recovery agencies', Compainies that collect and supply body parts for research. Since the UK's Human Tissue Act 2004 clarified the law, tissue recovery has become a lucrative and (mostly) legitimate industry, turning over millions of pounds a year.

It's not all abo though, the US Administration Biomedical Tis (BTS) to cease after accusatio parts had beer havested from New York, con relatives hadn obtained and t being screene BTS denies an

Pair of eyes £954

Scalp £380

Face nerve

£3

Oes

Trachea

£1,717

Thyroid & Parathyroid

£	
Amygdala	£954
Cerebellum	£318
Habenula	£1,131
Hippocampus	£1,131
Hypothalamus and Pituitary gland	£2085
Substantia Nigra	£954
Prefrontal Cortex	£954
Frontal Cortex	£318
Pineal gland	£954
Globus Pallidus	£954
Thalamus	£954
Total	**£10,707**

Brain

26**ESQUIRE**MAY 2007

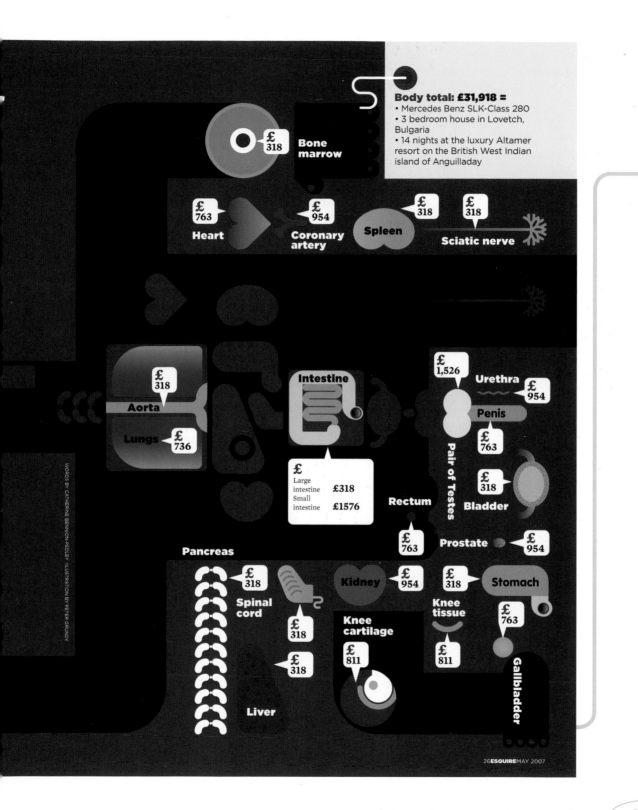

Body total: £31,918 =
• Mercedes Benz SLK-Class 280
• 3 bedroom house in Lovetch, Bulgaria
• 14 nights at the luxury Altamer resort on the British West Indian island of Anguilladay

GALAXY
Design by Paul Palmer-Edwards

Client: Quercus Publishing
Design firm: Grade Design
Typography: Paul Palmer-Edwards
Illustration: Paul Palmer-Edwards
and Jurgen Ziewe

An impressive array of photorealistic artist's impressions of the Milky Way and planetary vistas make up the core of the diagrammatic designs for *Galaxy* from Quercus Publishing. Each spread features different views of planets' surfaces, relationships to neighboring moons and stars, and size compared with other planets.

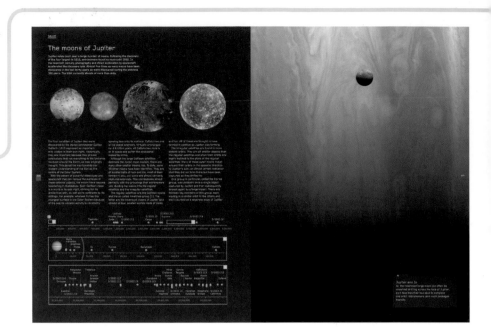

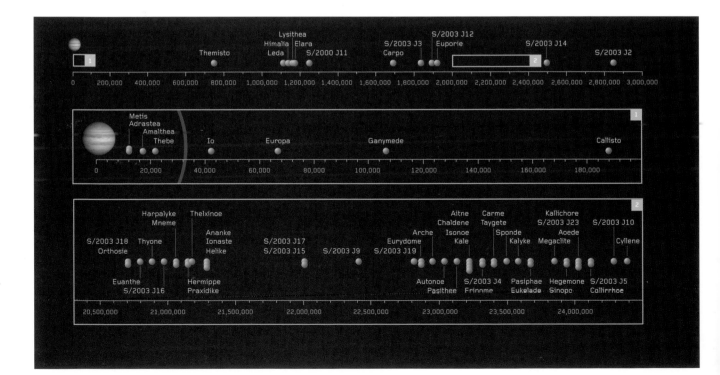

The proximity of the moons of Jupiter is shown in two ways: in a beautifully executed artist's impression, and as a three-tiered table that plots the vast distances between moons and planet.

reference

Paul Palmer-Edwards comments, "I took my reference from exploded images of astronomy, and used them to make clear visual sense of the distances involved, while giving the reader a photorealistic impression of space."

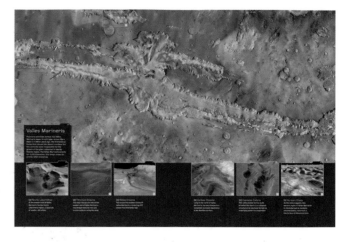

A photograph of the surface of Mars is used as the basis for another diagram that features exploded elevations of different areas of the planet's surface. These details are shown within green-keylined boxes that mimic the appearance of the tabbed index cards often seen within desktop filing systems.

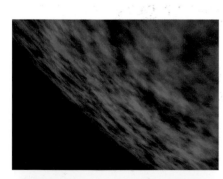

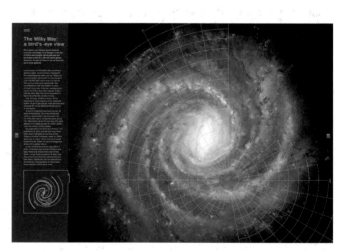

A diagram of the Milky Way is presented as a bird's-eye view, with its spiral formation clearly visible. This is overlaid with a bright-green web emanating from the Earth's sun that is used to indicate distances and degrees.

INDIEWOOD CHART
Design by Andy Smith

Client: *Sight & Sound* magazine
Design firm: Andy Smith
Art direction: Chris Brawn
Typography: Andy Smith
Illustration: Andy Smith

This diagram shows the connections between the new school of "indiewood" directors, producers, actors, and writers who work in the US movie industry, and the films they make. The name of each individual sits at the top of the diagram and is connected, via a complex mesh of colorful solid, dashed, and dotted lines, to a handwritten version of a film title. The location of the title denotes the year of production, which is clearly indicated by a list of dates, set in reverse chronological order, which runs up the left-hand side of this piece. The role of each individual is indicated by the style of line that connects their name to a film title—a solid line indicates actor, a dashed line denotes director, and a dotted line, writer.

reference

This is one of the projects in *Diagrams* that were inspired by the London Underground map, designed by Henry Beck in 1933.

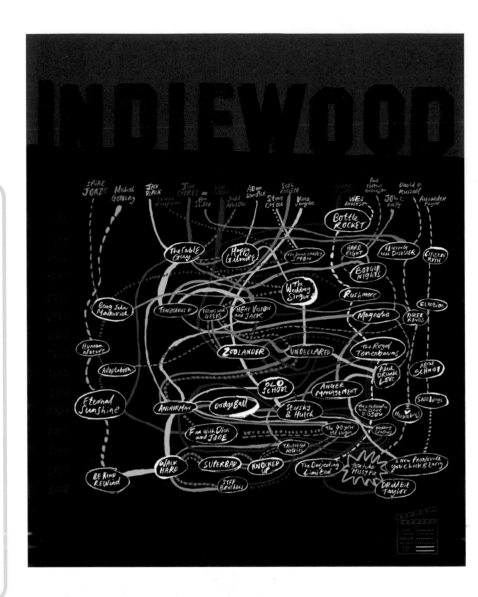

REINTERPRETING THE UNIVERSAL DECLARATION OF HUMAN RIGHTS
Design by Supriya Kalidas

Client: Jean-Benoît Lévy at the Academy of Art University, San Francisco
Design firm: Supriya Kalidas
Art direction: Supriya Kalidas

Supriya Kalidas' motivation for this project was her desire to create a greater understanding of and interest in the Universal Declaration of Human Rights. Her typographic design reorganizes the elements of the declaration into an easy-to-understand interactive version. It was designed for use in locations such as community centers and schools.

The text is arranged in six color-coded and layered sections that rotate and match up to reveal new information, and create new diagrams. On the base layer, each section features a recommended combination that is indicated by a line of colored dots which, when aligned with corresponding transparent circles on the upper disk, provide the reader with unexpected combinations.

reference

By selecting a colorful, interactive approach, her design engages its intended audience by reminding them of the experience of playing board games, and was itself inspired in part by the spinning element of the board game Twister.

LOVE WILL TEAR US APART
AGAIN POSTER
Design by Peter Crnokrak

Client: Design Supremo
Design firm: The Luxury of Protest
Art direction: Peter Crnokrak

This diagram plots the 85-plus recorded covers of Joy Division's "Love will Tear us Apart" in relation to the original 1980 release. Not only does it indicate the time since the original recording, it also shows the artist's name, the release name, the release date, and the label.

A basic radial structure is used to organize the cover versions in chronological order. A line of dots represents the number of recordings issued each year, thus allowing for a quick visual assessment of the increase in cover versions as time has progressed. Artists who have capitalized on their recording the most (by rereleasing their cover versions) are also shown—curved lines join one version to the next. The radial structure of the diagram enables these complex relationships to be represented efficiently, and to be more easily accessed than a regular linear structure would have allowed.

reference

Peter Crnokrak describes his inspiration for the project as "an interest in the song itself, and its place of honor in music history. With regard to Crnokrak's visual inspiration, readers can see the influence of images of solar eclipses and the manner in which the sun's rays radiate out from behind the moon.

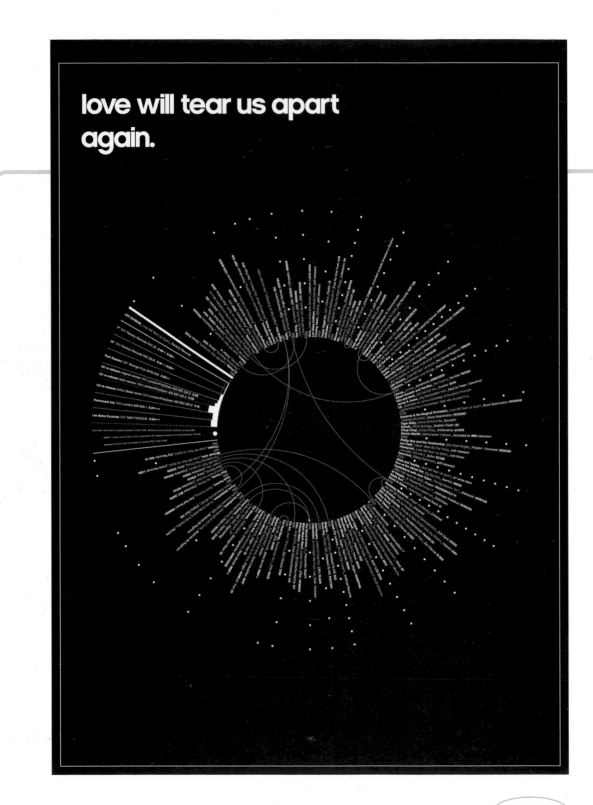

SHELL BOARD GAME
Design by Eelco van den Berg

Client: Shell
Design firm: Eelco van den Berg
Art direction: Francel Verlaat

The aim of this board game is to educate the players about driving economically. "It's a playful way of teaching," says Eelco van den Berg. The board itself comes folded into quarters in its packaging; when opened out, a spiral, numbered pathway is revealed. Each division features an image, with 10 hazardous driving situations on special orange warning squares.

reference

There are a number of examples of game designs within the pages of this book—this is the second featured piece to be inspired by "the game of the goose" (see MAKI's design for Bij Jansen on pages 16 and 17).

HEART DIAGRAM
Design by Joel Katz and David E. Schpok

Client: The Ovations Press
Design firm: Joel Katz Design Associates
Art direction: Joel Katz
Illustration: Joel Katz and
    David E. Schpok

Featured in the book *Heart Diseases and Cardiovascular Health*, this diagram shows the blood's route through the heart and lungs, and how it feeds the body. Joel Katz's aim with this design was to "transcend the anatomy and appearance of the heart to emphasize its function."

reference

The aorta, superior and inferior vena cava, veins, and arteries are visualized almost as if they are roads at a complex intersection, weaving under and over each other in order to carry their biological traffic to its destination.

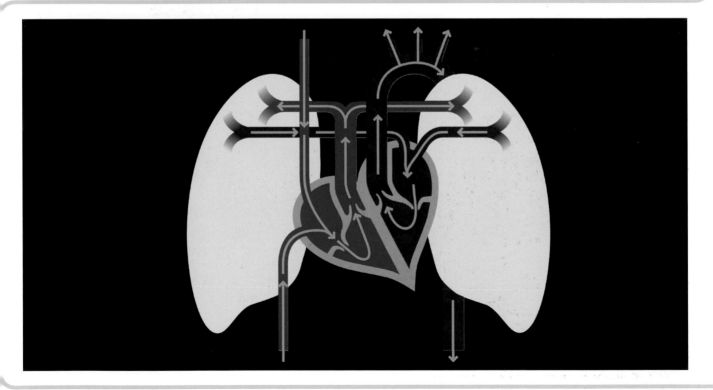

H-AND-S EMPTY + H-AND-S FULL
Design by Jean-Benoît Lévy

Client: Self-initiated
Design firm: Studio A N D
Art direction: Jean-Benoît Lévy
Typography: Moonkyung Choi,
and Sylvestre Lucia
Illustration: Diana Stoen

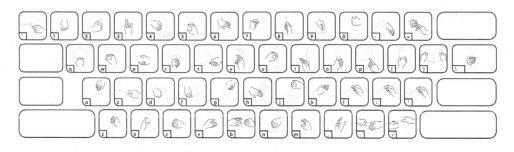

GESTURES AND INSTRUCTIONS

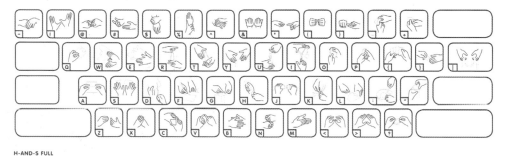

H-AND-S FULL

Figure for US keyboard, above: "normal" / below: "shift"   Copyright: 2006 / www.and.ch   Available at: www.myfonts.com/?refby=and

Hand signs are known mostly as a system of communication for people with a hearing impairment, but Studio A N D recognized the usefulness of hand-sign images within graphic design. This collection of individual symbols can be brought together to create diagrams that transcend language and communicate effectively.

reference

The inspiration behind this exciting design concept was the tiny, detailed diagrams intended to instruct a diner on how to eat with a pair of chopsticks, as found on the back of a chopstick package.

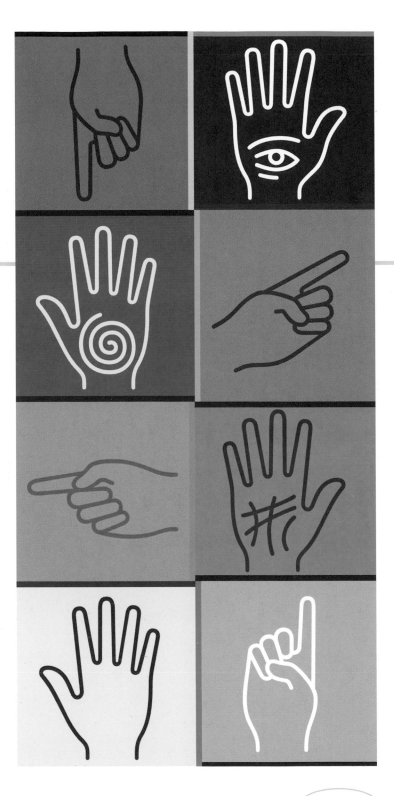

COUNTER CLOCK
Design by Emmanuel Prado

Client: University of Buenos Aires,
Faculty of Architecture, Design,
and Urbanism

For this project for the University of
Buenos Aires in Argentina, different
levels of text, varying shapes, curved
lines, straight lines, and large letterforms
come together in a vibrant diagram
that describes the design process of
a particular project, from conception
to finished design. Prado begins by
tracking the journey undertaken to
develop the initial concept. The curved
lines in his layout represent tension and
setbacks, and these are clearly evident
at this stage.

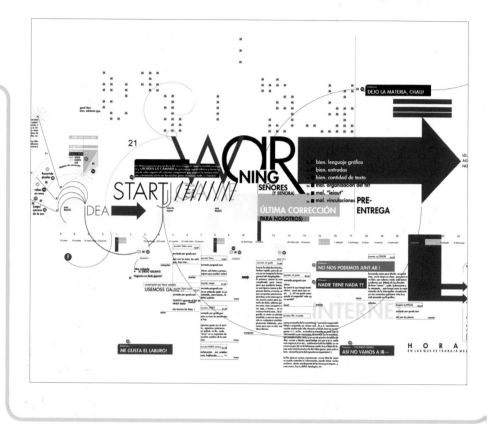

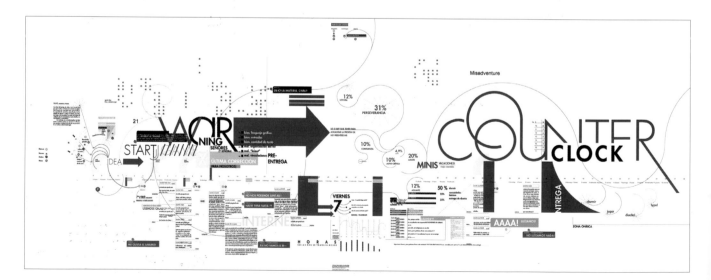

He plots the times, dates, and locations that are integral to the whole process, as well as the moods that affect his progress. Although the design as a whole reads from left to right, the viewer is led in many directions to appreciate the abundance of situations that influence the design process. Prado says his main aim was "to analyze and express chaos as the primary component of ideas generation, and to link this concept to the real world in which you find lots of situations that mold and directly affect a project."

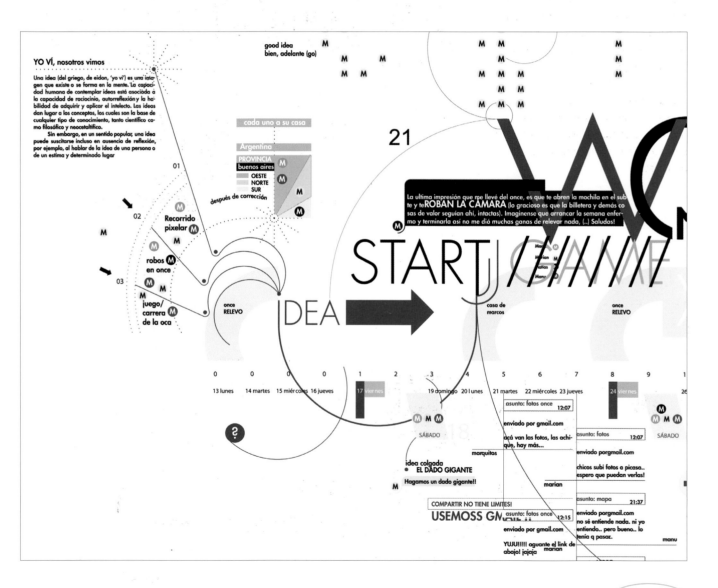

It is clear that Prado drew inspiration and themes from the circular forms of his chosen lightweight sans-serif typeface. Circular elements are found throughout the complex design of Counter Clock. They are used to link elements, form icons, soften the corners of text boxes, and form the peaks and troughs within graphs.

q e u o p

a d g c b

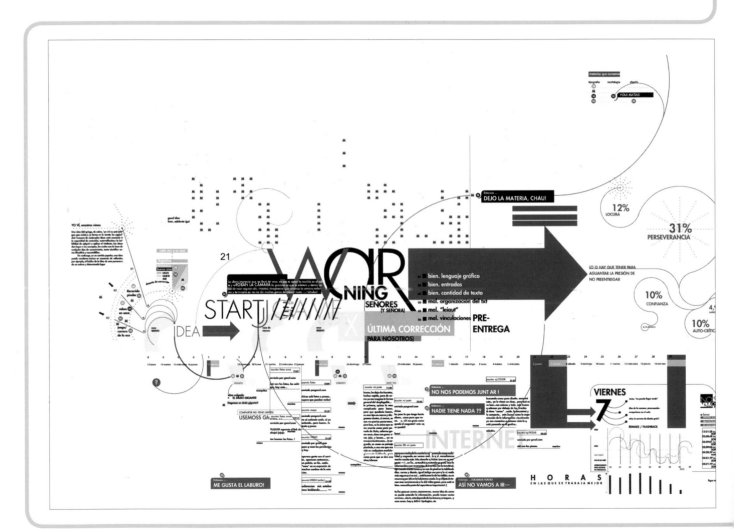

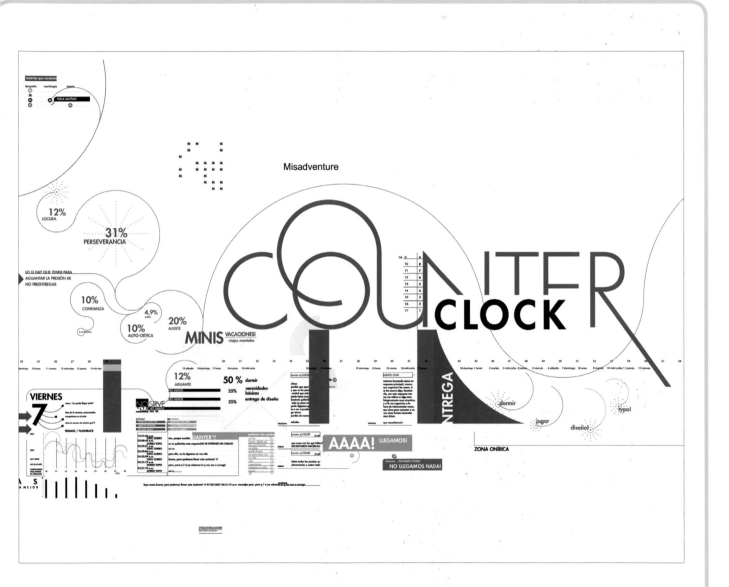

Misadventure

GLOBAL VILLAGE
Design by Sebastian Gagin

Client: University of Buenos Aires, Faculty of Architecture, Design, and Urbanism

Gagin's predominantly typographic composition, entitled Global Village (Aldea Global), plots the historic context and globalization of Once, in Buenos Aires, Argentina. The piece is structured to visually express the way in which trends and events have gradually evolved to produce the congestion and chaos that is characteristic of the area today. Scattered topics lead the viewer to massed blocks of information, butting up to one another, and reading in no particular order. "It is comprised of plain texts, definitions, charts, comparisons, Internet forums, statistics, chronologies, etc.," says Gagin, who intends the viewer to create his or her own personal text by sequencing the information as they choose.

Significant historic milestones are detailed, with particular emphasis placed on 1789 when Argentina achieved liberty and equal rights for all men, just after the Bastille, in Paris, France, had been taken.

A wide range of both past and present statistics is documented, including levels of unemployment, influences of fashion trends, people's hopes and dreams. Different visual interpretations separate each section, and although only two colors—red and blue—are used, varying tints provide many options for type to be overprinted or reversed out.

reference

This piece was inspired by hypertexts, where every word is linked to another word in a different text, enabling readers to make up a new, personal text by taking pieces and jumping from one text to another.

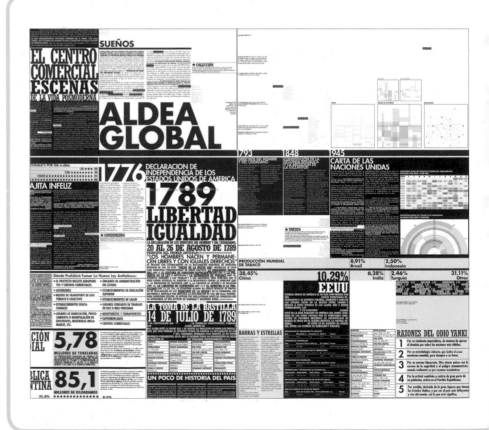

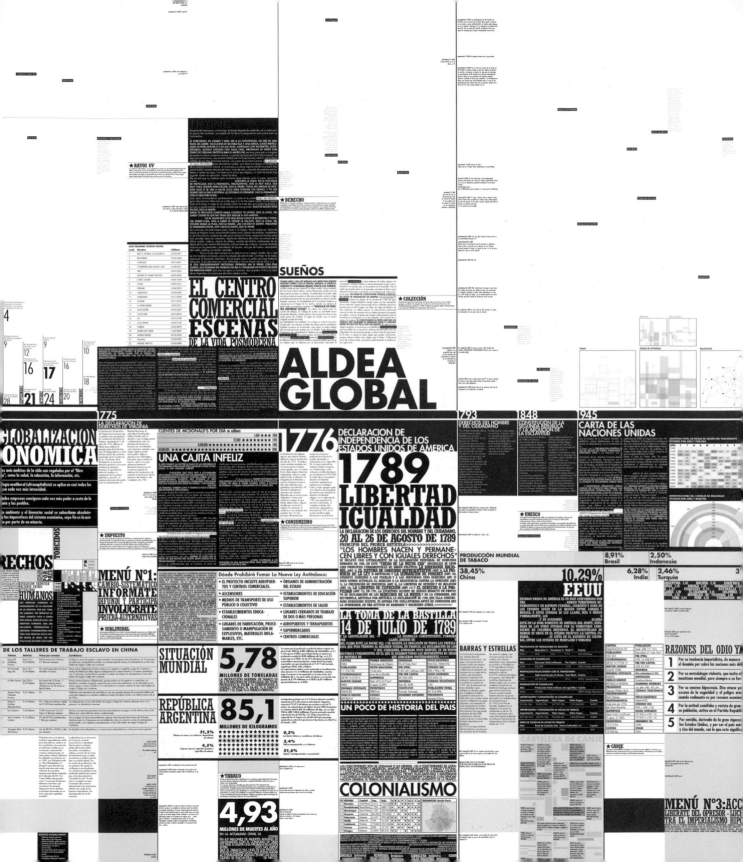

★ RAYOS UV

★ DERECHO

SUEÑOS

EL CENTRO COMERCIAL
ESCENAS DE LA VIDA POSMODERNA

★ COLECCIÓN

ALDEA GLOBAL

GLOBALIZACION ECONOMICA

775
LA DECLARACIÓN DE DERECHOS DE VIRGINIA

1776
DECLARACION DE INDEPENDENCIA DE LOS ESTADOS UNIDOS DE AMERICA

1789
LIBERTAD
IGUALDAD

LA DECLARACIÓN DE LOS DERECHOS DEL HOMBRE Y DEL CIUDADANO, 20 AL 26 DE AGOSTO DE 1789
PRINCIPIO DEL PRIMER ARTÍCULO:
"LOS HOMBRES NACEN Y PERMANE-CEN LIBRES Y CON IGUALES DERECHOS"

1793
DERECHOS DEL HOMBRE Y DEL CIUDADANO

1848
CONSTITUCION DE LA SEGUNDA REPUBLICA Y LA ABOLICION DE...

1945
CARTA DE LAS NACIONES UNIDAS

LA TOMA DE LA BASTILLA
14 DE JULIO DE 1789

★ UNESCO

★ IMPUESTO

★ CONSUMISMO

DERECHOS HUMANOS
TORCIDOS

MENÚ Nº1:
CAMBIO SISTEMÁTICO
INFORMATE
DIFUNDÍ Y PARTICIPÁ
INVOLUCRATE
PRUEBA ALTERNATIVAS

★ SUBLIMINAL

UNA CAJITA INFELIZ

CLIENTES DE MCDONALD'S POR DÍA

Dónde Prohibirá Fumar La Nueva Ley Antitabaco:
- EL PROYECTO INCLUYE AEROPUER-TOS Y CENTROS COMERCIALES.
- ASCENSORES
- MEDIOS DE TRANSPORTE DE USO PÚBLICO O COLECTIVO
- ESTABLECIMIENTOS EDUCA-CIONALES
- LUGARES DE FABRICACIÓN, PROCE-SAMIENTO O MANIPULACIÓN DE EXPLOSIVOS, MATERIALES INFLA-MABLES, ETC.
- ÓRGANOS DE ADMINISTRACIÓN DEL ESTADO
- ESTABLECIMIENTOS DE EDUCACIÓN SUPERIOR
- ESTABLECIMIENTOS DE SALUD
- LUGARES CERRADOS DE TRABAJO DE DOS O MÁS PERSONAS
- AEROPUERTOS Y TERRAPUERTOS
- SUPERMERCADOS
- CENTROS COMERCIALES

DE LOS TALLERES DE TRABAJO ESCLAVO EN CHINA

SITUACIÓN MUNDIAL
5,78
MILLONES DE TONELADAS

REPÚBLICA ARGENTINA
85,1
MILLONES DE KILOGRAMOS

★ TABACO

4,93
MILLONES DE MUERTES AL AÑO

PRODUCCIÓN MUNDIAL DE TABACO

38,45% China	10,29% EEUU	8,91% Brasil	6,28% India	2,50% Indonesia	2,46% Turquia	3...

EEUU

BARRAS Y ESTRELLAS

UN POCO DE HISTORIA DEL PAÍS

CARTELERA DE CANJE

★ CANJE

COLONIALISMO

RAZONES DEL ODIO Y...

1 Por su tendencia imperialista, de manera el dominio por sobre las naciones más débiles.
2 Por su metodología violenta, que incita el mantiene mundial, pero siempre a su fa...
3 Por su enorme hipocresía. Dice atacar el exceso de la seguridad y el peligro extern cuando realmente es por razones económ...
4 Por la actitud xenófoba y racista de gran su población, activa en el Partido Republi...
5 Por envidia, derivada de la gran riqueza los Estados Unidos, y por ser el país más y rico del mundo, con lo que esto signific...

MENÚ Nº3: ACC...
LIBERATE DEL OPRESOR - LUC...
TRA EL IMPERIALISMO HIP...

TRAFALGAR STAMPS PRESENTATION PACK AND POSTMARKS
Design by Peter Dawson and Tom Green

Client: Royal Mail
Design firm: Grade Design
Art direction: Peter Dawson
Typography: Peter Dawson and Tom Green
Illustration: Tom Green

The Trafalgar Stamps presentation pack incorporates a number of diagrams that tell the story of the Battle of Trafalgar. The front of the pack shows a day on board the British warship HMS *Victory*, on the eve of battle, and includes a diagram portraying the formation of fighting ships. The reverse of the pack shows the impact of the battle on Britain's culture.

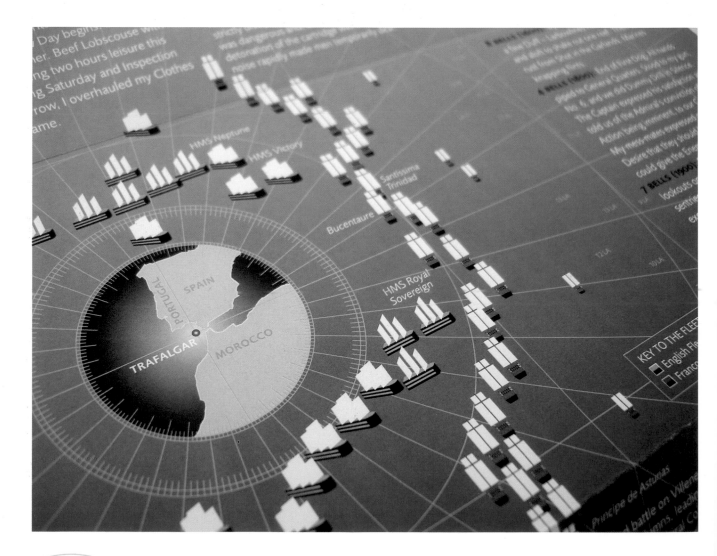

Dawson and Green were influenced by the design of sea charts and maps, which themselves are informed by cartographic styles of the past, incorporating elaborate crests, graduated measurement scales, and other navigational details.

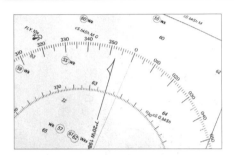

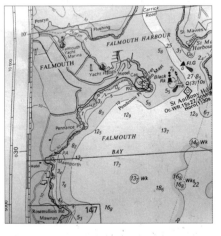

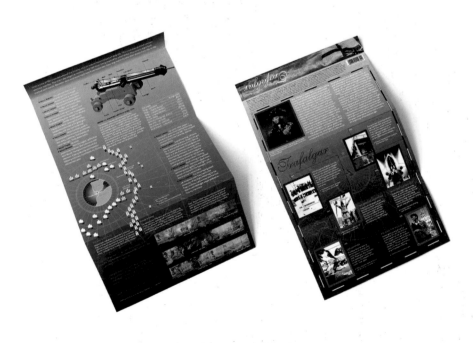

BRITVIC ANNUAL REPORT
Design by Peter Grundy

Client: Luminous Design
Design firm: Grundini Ltd.
Art direction: John Towell
Typography: Peter Grundy
Illustration: Peter Grundy

This Britvic design was created by Peter Grundy to lighten the experience of reading what is often a complex annual report. In classic Grundy style, this design explains how Britvic make their soft drinks, from growing and picking fruit to recycling packaging. This diagram makes good use of bright colors, simplified shapes and curves, repetition, and amusing, lighthearted detail, such as a curved cargo ship and four bendy trucks.

reference

Grundy's inspiration for this piece was 3D, axonometric road maps. Containers, trees, buildings, and methods of transportation rise from the colorful Britvic production route in parallel perspective.

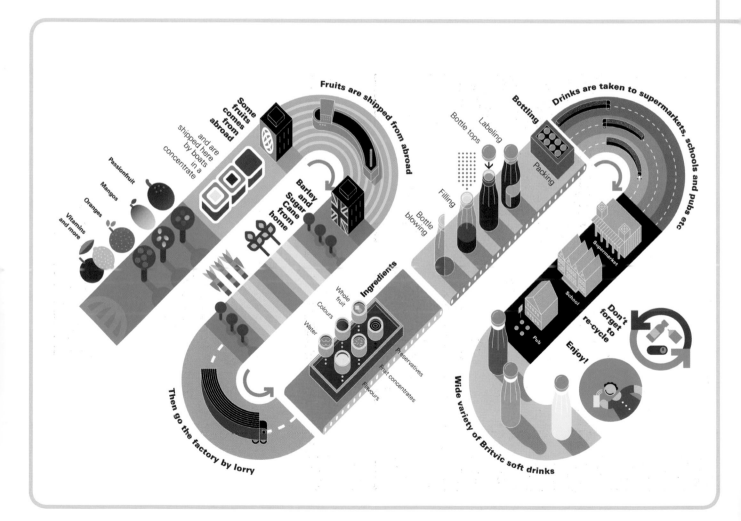

SEQUENCE OF OPENING A CAN
Design by Tae Koo

Client: Claudia Dallendörfer and Jean-
    Benoît Lévy
Illustration: Tae Koo

Korean designer Tae Koo uses a sequence of photographic images to indicate how to open a food can, without any written text. "Images can be more powerful than words in delivering information. I wanted to create an interactive piece that people can understand easily even if they don't know any English, or any other language," says Tae Koo.

reference

Sequential photographic imagery has long been used as an effective way to demonstrate function. Examples of this can be found stretching right back to the early days of photography, in the work of photographic pioneer Eadweard Muybridge. Perhaps best known for capturing movement within a sequence of photographs, Muybridge's work still influences the designs of many artists and designers looking to communicate a chronology of events to an international audience.

PERSONAL GRAPHIC DIARY
Design by Andrés Celesia

Client: University of Buenos Aires,
Faculty of Architecture, Design,
and Urbanism

These diagrams analyze bus journeys
to a bookstore, and a robbery that took
place after one of these. They form
a graphic diary of a particular period
when the designer was traveling to and
from Once, in Buenos Aires, Argentina.
This diary shows the different routes
taken and the observations the designer
made, giving a very personal insight
into the day-to-day activities of the
area. For example, the section with
the red background expresses a five-
minute conversation the designer's
friend Julieta had with the owner of
a flower stall. It traces nine subjects,
showing how they interrelate, and what
kind of language is used.

The diary concludes with the designer's
friend Maria being robbed. The blue
and black diagrams detail the money
involved, the location of the bookstore
and the thieves, and Maria's bad luck
with timing. The main caption in the
blue diagram is shown as a mirror image,
as Maria is talking to herself, asking
how she is coping with the robbery and
willing herself to remain strong and keep
calm. This visual story communicates
far more than words alone could achieve.

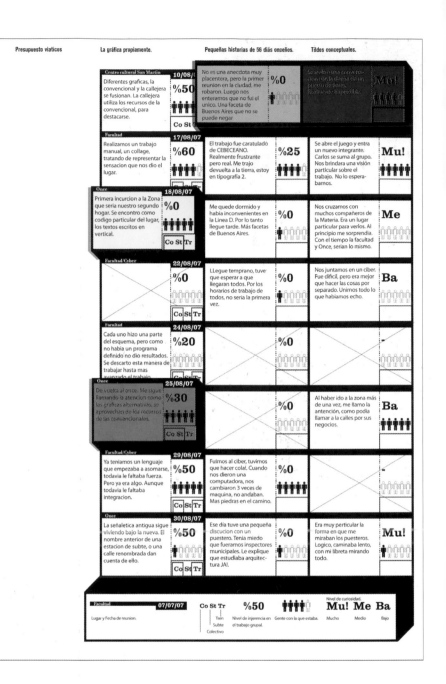

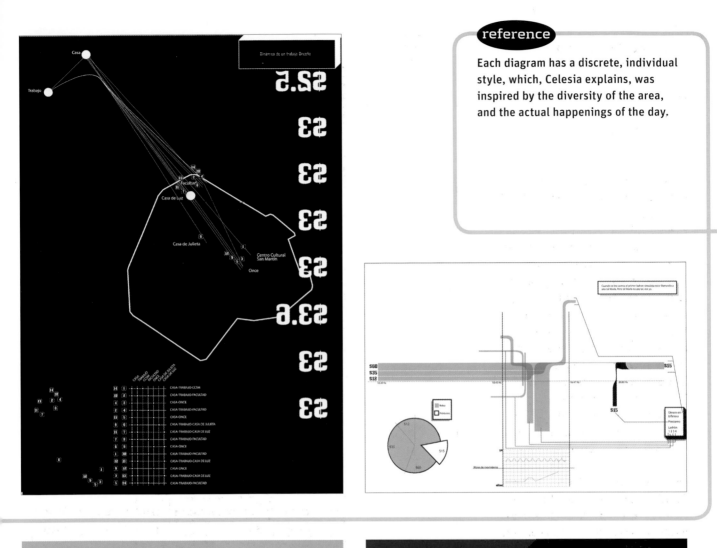

Each diagram has a discrete, individual style, which, Celesia explains, was inspired by the diversity of the area, and the actual happenings of the day.

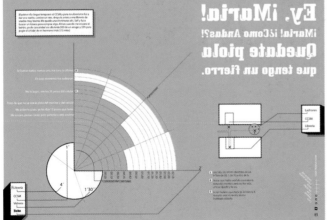

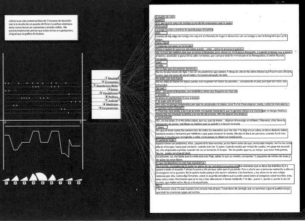

NATIONAL JOINT
INJECTION CONFERENCE
Design by Louise Carrier

Client: Dr. Robin Chakraverty
Design firm: Louise Carrier Graphic
   Design and Illustration
Art direction: Louise Carrier and
   Dr. Robin Chakraverty
Typography: Louise Carrier
Illustration: Louise Carrier

These diagrams are anatomical and clinical presentations of painful joint conditions that can be treated effectively by injections. Each image provides a detailed view of subcutaneous parts of the body, showing muscles, tendons, bones, and veins, all in cross section.

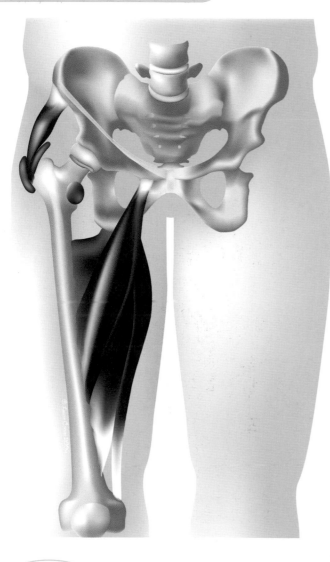
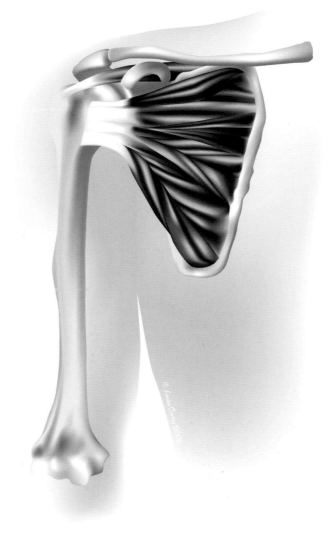

DIAGRAMS: Innovative Solutions for Graphic Designers

On the sources of her inspiration Louise Carrier comments, "In terms of look and feel, my life-drawing pastel work was a strong influence, as was *Scientific American* magazine, and the work of Yoshitaka Amano was a huge inspiration. The particular image of great influence to me is from his work for the TV animation *Battle of the Planets! G-Force*."

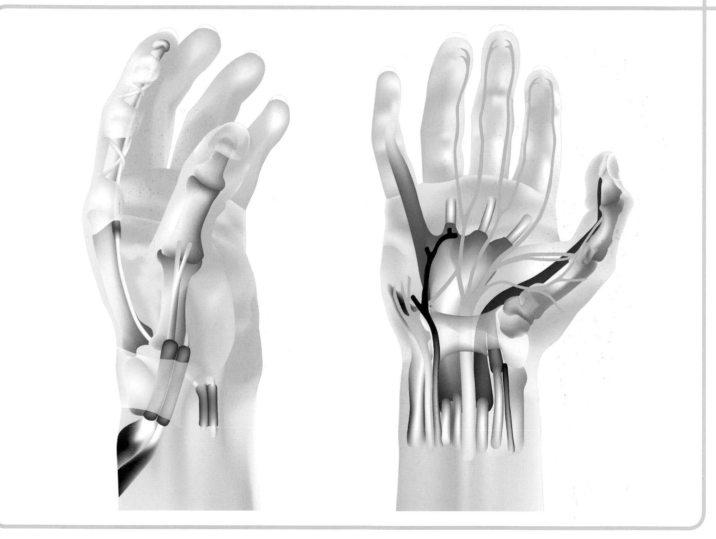

URBAN ATLAS

Design by Andrés Celesia, Matias Gigliotti, Luz Arias, and Julieta Vaggi

Client: University of Buenos Aires, Faculty of Architecture, Design, and Urbanism

This detailed diagram informs the viewer about a popular district of Argentina's capital, Buenos Aires—El Barrio de Once. Tints of just three colors are used to group elements and create hierarchies, with varying weights of rules added to frame and link sections. Although there are a number of individual tables and charts within the design, a visual cohesion is created because each section is arranged around a fairly dominant horizontal bar of words butting up to one another.

Information regarding the historic growth of the area is also given. Diagrams show how places are linked with transport, and how streets relate to each other.

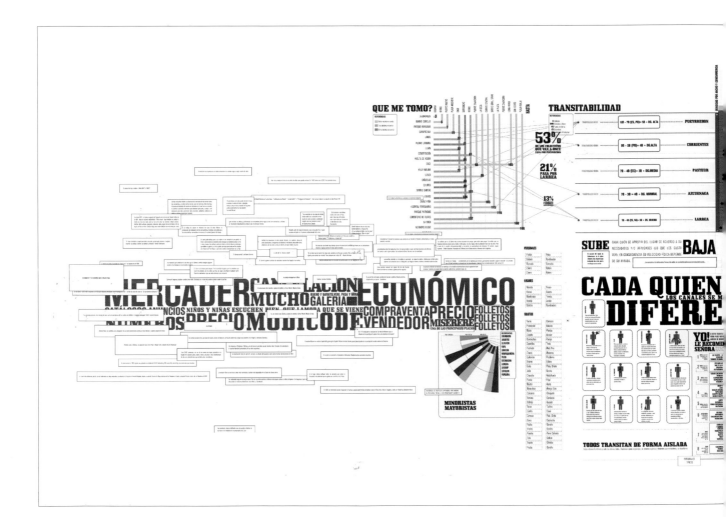

Typical activities are identified, from stallholders selling such goods as the well-known bread of the area, to people handing out leaflets or calling out to passersby to draw them into local venues. Prostitutes are noted, along with sightseers. People from neighboring districts who visit only at weekends or on holidays are listed; they go to shop or chat with friends, or merely to buy a newspaper. However, shoppers are the most prominent, and one diagram analyzes the kind of shopping that generally occurs, suggesting that it is mostly people buying gifts or ladies' clothes who frequent the area.

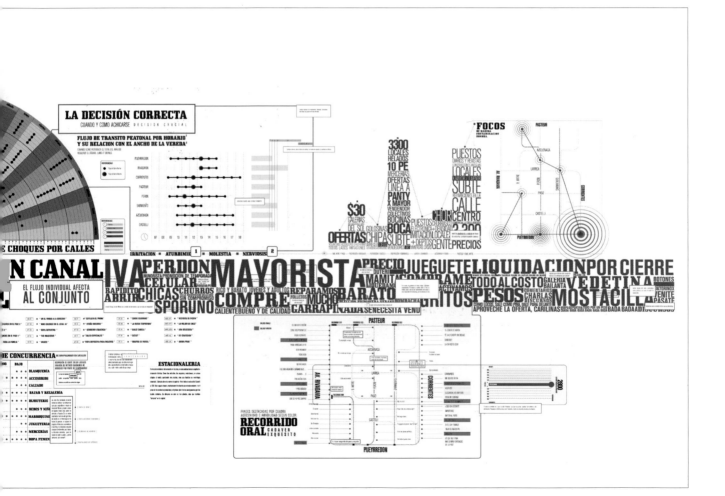

The lively street scenes and inhabitants of El Barrio de Once were the inspiration for this piece. The designers adopted the graphic language, colors, and textures prevalent in the neighborhood for this "atlas."

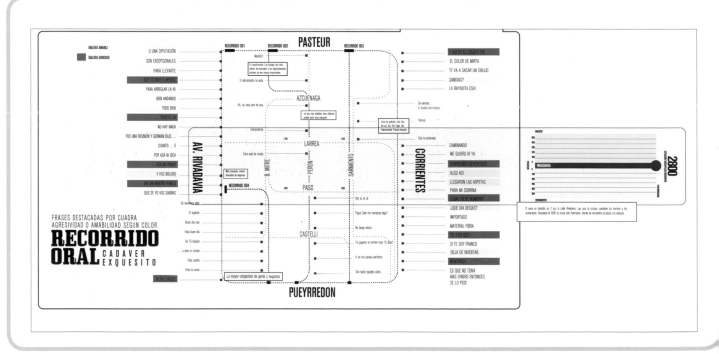

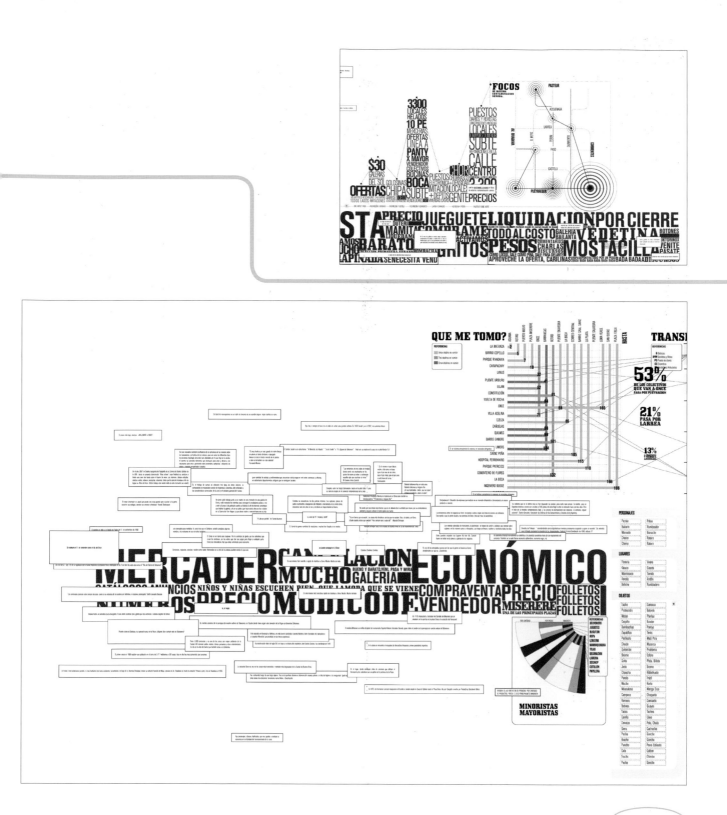

SAVE FUEL ADVERTISEMENT
Design by Peter Grundy

Client: Mark Reddy, Art Director
at BMP DDB
Design firm: Grundini Ltd.
Typography: Peter Grundy
Illustration: Peter Grundy

Peter Grundy has designed this piece to work on two levels. At first glance, it is clear that VW cars save fuel and money, but in addition, on a micro level, each letter that makes up this diagram contains more detailed typographic and diagrammatic information that explains how the VW engine fulfills this task. Each large, individual letter is cleverly used to accommodate at least one relevant informative icon.

reference

Technical manuals and the style of icons and illustrations typical of such manuals were the inspiration behind this piece.

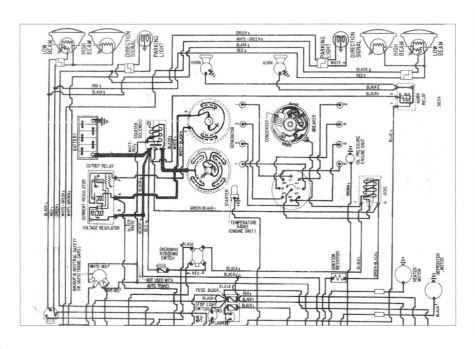

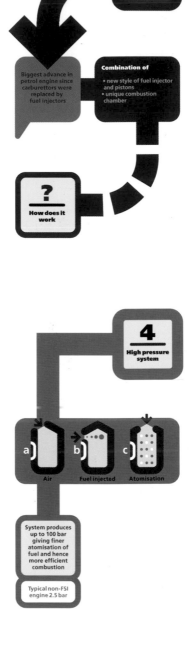

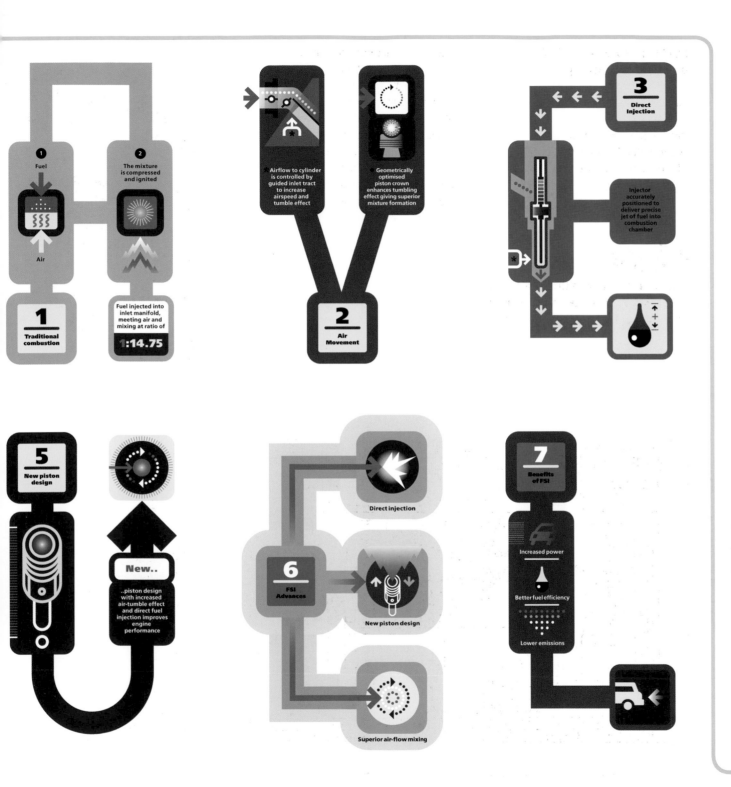

1 Traditional combustion

① Fuel
Air

2 The mixture is compressed and ignited

Fuel injected into inlet manifold, meeting air and mixing at ratio of **1:14.75**

2 Air Movement

Airflow to cylinder is controlled by guided inlet tract to increase airspeed and tumble effect

Geometrically optimised piston crown enhances tumbling effect giving superior mixture formation

3 Direct Injection

Injector accurately positioned to deliver precise jet of fuel into combustion chamber

5 New piston design

New..

..piston design with increased air-tumble effect and direct fuel injection improves engine performance

6 FSI Advances

Direct injection

New piston design

Superior air-flow mixing

7 Benefits of FSI

Increased power

Better fuel efficiency

Lower emissions

GAME ONCE
Design by Marcos Farina, Emmanuel Prado, and Mariana Sequeira

Client: University of Buenos Aires, Faculty of Architecture, Design, and Urbanism

This project is a graphic interpretation of the daily routines of deliverymen in the Once neighborhood of Buenos Aires, Argentina. "Once is a rather small neighborhood filled with shops, people, traffic, and noise. There are inhabitants from many cultures, engaged in many activities, and there are lots of deliverymen," say the designers, who find the frenetic comings and goings of these people amusing and fun. The locals' lives remind them of board games where there is a starting point, a destination, and various influences and obstacles en route.

A tremendous amount of detail is conveyed in this piece. For example, in the tabular matter running horizontally on the right of the diagram (and in the detail below), deliveries of different types of clothing are listed according to the days of the week; destinations are given along with any obstacles encountered on the way, such as trees, posts, telephones, parking meters, and pedestrians. Even such dangers as holes in the road and bumping into elderly ladies are noted. Both the design and the use of language in this diagram capture the hustle and bustle of Once and give the viewer a realistic insight into its character.

reference

All the neighborhood information is laid out in colors, typefaces, and configurations that emulate video-game screens, capturing their vitality; individual words and phrases applicable to both the gaming world and delivery-men's lives are highlighted; and one section is constructed as though it were a slot machine.

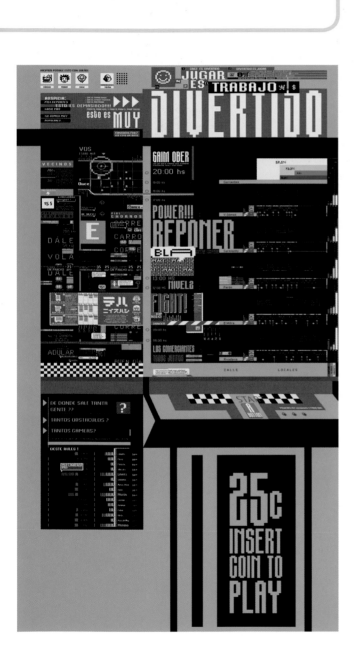

LES DÉLICES
Design by Pierre Sponchiado

Client: Self-initiated
Design firm: Bornstein & Sponchiado
Art direction: Pierre Sponchiado
Illustration: Pierre Sponchiado
Photography: Pierre Sponchiado

The objective of Les Délices (The Delights) was to establish a graphic vocabulary for taste. "We have dissected the different elements that make up taste and created one family of pictograms that represent olfactory sensations, another that conveys details of the substance of a particular food, and finally, a series of pictograms that represent the four primary flavors," says Pierre Sponchiado. The four flavors are bitter, acid, sweet, and salty. By bringing their iconic representations of flavor together with those that convey the texture and aroma of a particular food item, Bornstein & Sponchiado were able to create a visual code with possible applications across areas including catering, restaurants, packaging, and the world of wine.

This intriguing graphic code can be used effectively by itself, or as a supplement to photography or even illustration. The featured examples of Les Délices "in action" make very clever, considered use of expert photography and art direction in order to enhance the meaning of Pierre Sponchiado's icons.

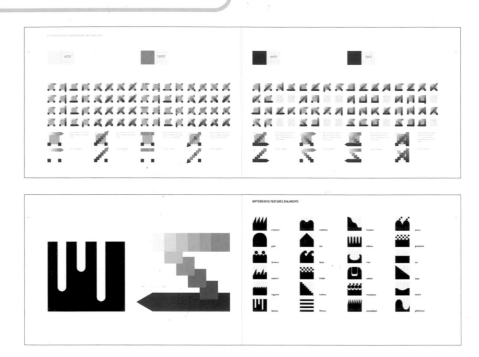

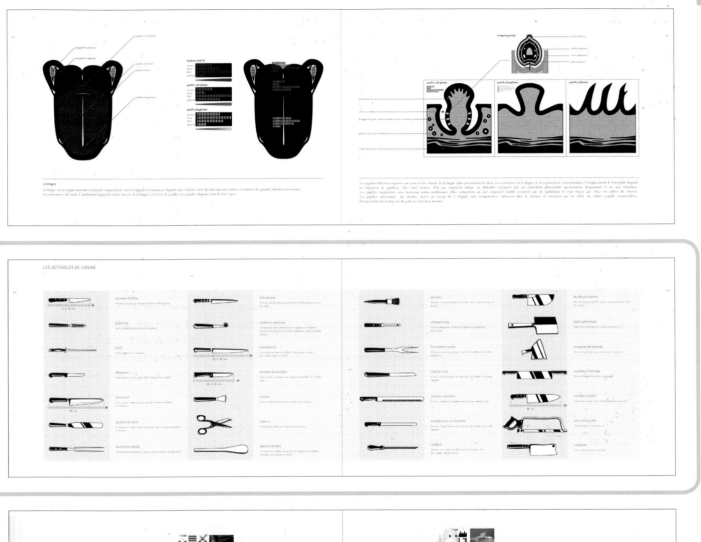

La langue

La langue est un organe musculeux corporel comportant le muscle lingual et la muqueuse linguale qui s'enroure entre les faisceaux musculaires et contient des glandes salivaires accessoires, des vaisseaux et des nerfs. L'épithélium lingual de la face dorsale de la langue est hérissé de papilles. Les papilles linguales sont de trois types.

Les papilles filiformes réparties sur toute la face dorsale de la langue (plus précisément les deux tiers antérieurs de la langue, le tiers postérieur se correspondant à l'emplacement de l'amygdale linguale est dépourvu de papilles), elles sont formées d'un axe conjonctif unique ou dédoublé recouvert par un épithélium pluristratifié pavimenteux desquamant et en pue kératinise. Les papilles fongiformes sont beaucoup moins nombreuses. Elles composent un axe conjonctif ramifié recouvert par un épithélium de type buccal qui coiffe les saillies du chorion. Les papilles caliciformes, au desure, situées au niveau du V lingual, sont volumineuses, enfoncées dans le chorion et entourées par un sillon au culture (papille circumvallée), elles possèdent des bourgeons du goût sur leurs faces latérales.

LES USTENSILES DE CUISINE

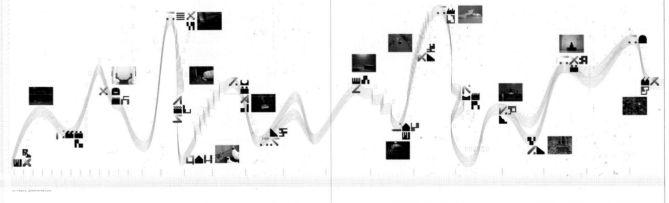

"Pourtant, comme toujours en pareilles circonstances, j'avais envie de demander plus de détails, de questionner comme un mioche : Et c'est bon comment ? S'il vous plaît, dites-moi ce qui est bon! Quand ça pénètre dans la bouche? Quand les dents entrent en action? Quand c'est sur la langue? Dans la gorge? Avant? Après? Tout le temps? Et le lendemain, dites-moi, quand vous y repensez, est-ce que ce n'est pas encore meilleur?"

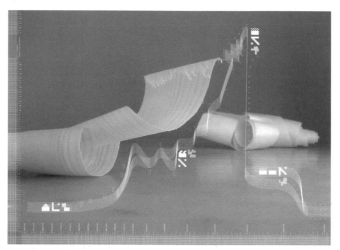

The complex inspiration behind the design approach for this project clearly comes from a number of sources, including the swashes and curves of Islamic calligraphy.

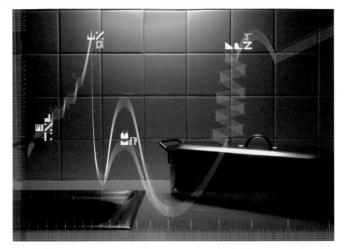

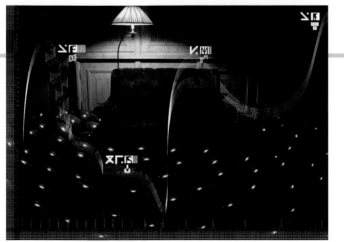

CITY ON A PLATE
Design by Jennifer Cosgrove

Client: Self-initiated
Design firm: notNeutral
President CEO: Chiaki Kanda
Photography: Julie Toy

notNeutral portrayed 16 diverse cities on sets of 30cm (12in) plates. Each set of four plates has a particular conceptual framework that relates the four cities featured to each other as a means of investigating cultural, economic, historical, and political impact on the mapped area. The cities are shown in a graphic language of line, color, and pattern.

Melbourne

reference

The inspiration behind these designs comes from the environmental design and urban planning work produced by notNeutral's sister company Rios Clementi Hale Studios. Each city's core is printed on a black background, with key buildings represented by orange icons, and rivers and public spaces shown in blue and green, respectively. The dramatic white band on the Berlin plate marks where the Berlin wall once stood.

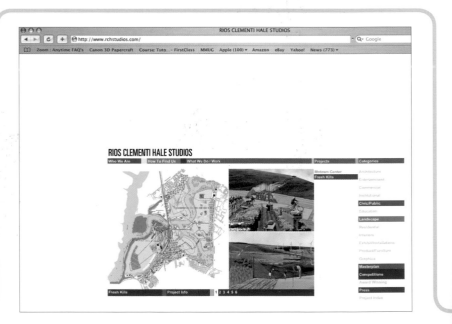

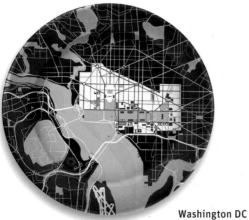

Washington DC

Berlin

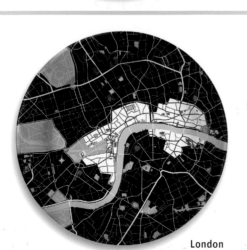

London

Brasilia

Cairo

Dubai

INTERNATIONAL SCHOOL
BASEL PROSPECTUS
**Design by Paula Benson and
Claire Warner**

Client: International School Basel
Design firm: Form
Art direction: Paula Benson
and Paul West
Illustration: Claire Warner
Photography: Kate Martin
Copywriting: Richard West

This map is from the prospectus of The International School Basel, Switzerland. Form's design, which uses fluorescent yellow ink to mimic the effect of a highlighter pen, appeals to both students and parents alike.

The map is divided into three sections that show: 1) the overall map of Europe; 2) the location and comparative size of Switzerland within Europe; and 3) the comparative size of Basel and the location of the school.

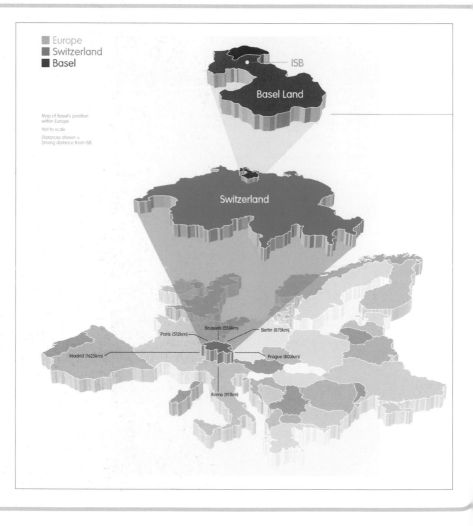

TRANSIT HEART
Design by Joel Katz

Client: Self-initiated
Design firm: Joel Katz Design
   Associates
Art direction: Joel Katz
Typography: Joel Katz

Joel Katz's design is a "biological map." Katz says, "I have always believed that function is independent of appearance, whether it is biological networks or transportation networks. As Richard Wurman [a pioneer in the field of information architecture] said, 'people only understand something in relation to something they already understand,' so I've developed a notation based on familiar functions that many people already understand."

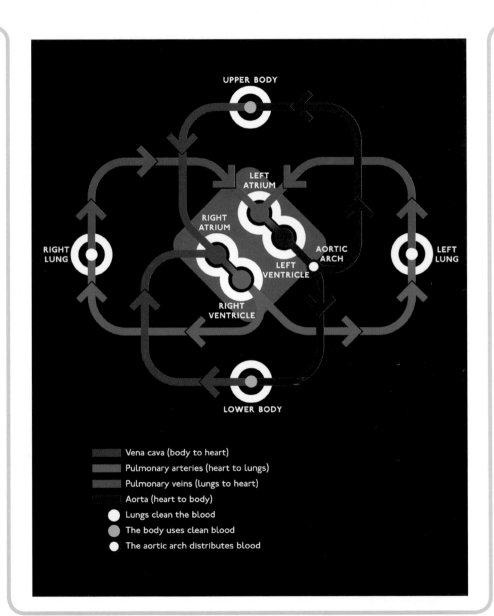

TYPOGRAPHIC TABLE
Design by Ridhi Sain

Client: Self-initiated
Design firm: Coley Porter Bell
Art direction: Ridhi Sain

Ridhi Sain's typographic table is a simple, effective, educational tool that classifies, systematizes, and compares some of the most commonly used fonts. This table lists the name of each font along with the name of the original typographer/ designer and the year in which it was designed. It also shows a sample of the font.

reference

Ridhi comments, "Having taken inspiration from the periodic table, designed by the Russian chemist Dmitry Mendeleev in 1869, my design is a confluence of art and science. It integrates various typefaces into a single structure that has been systematically arranged according to type family along the X axis and time line along the Y axis."

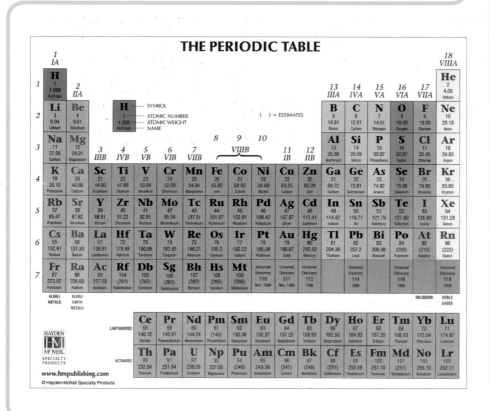

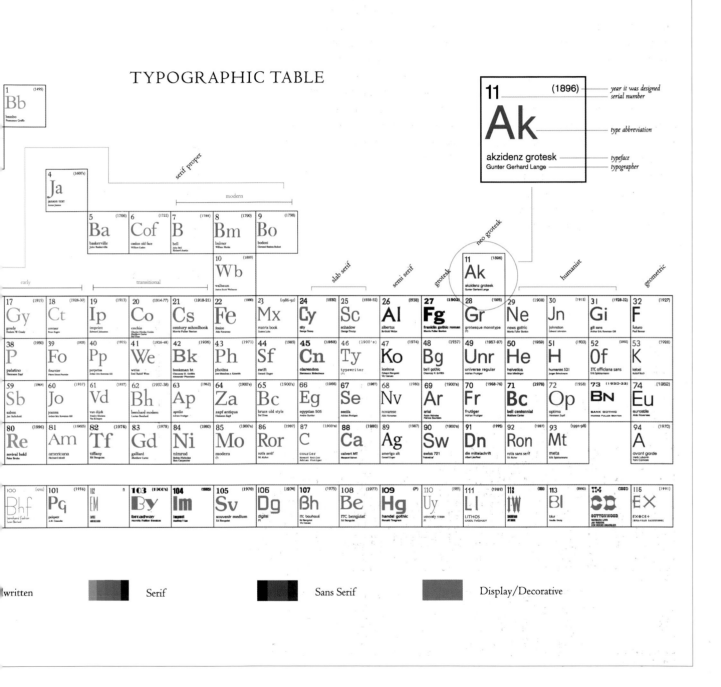

TYPOGRAPHIC TABLE

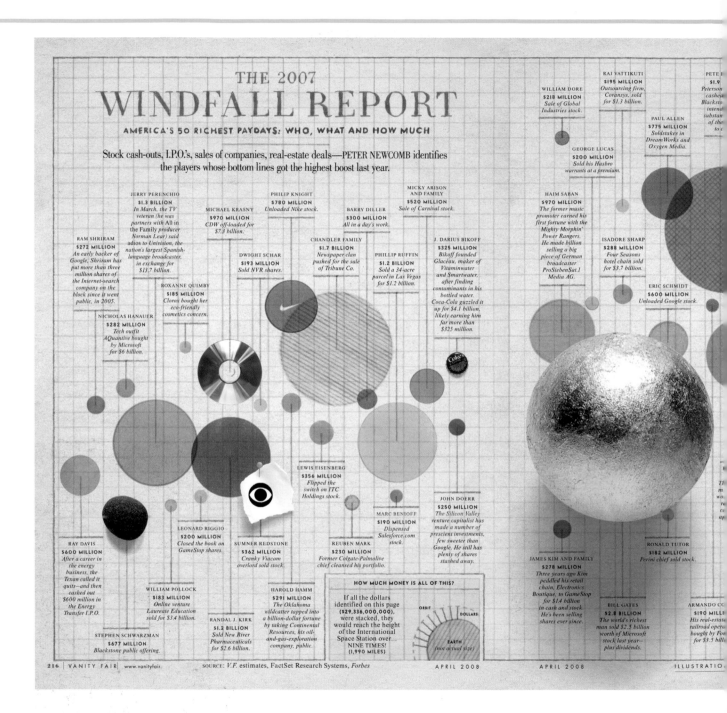

THE 2007
WINDFALL REPORT

AMERICA'S 50 RICHEST PAYDAYS: WHO, WHAT AND HOW MUCH

Stock cash-outs, I.P.O.'s, sales of companies, real-estate deals—PETER NEWCOMB identifies
the players whose bottom lines got the highest boost last year.

WILLIAM DORE
$218 MILLION
Sale of Global
Industries stock.

RAJ VATTIKUTI
$195 MILLION
Outsourcing firm,
Covansys, sold
for $1.3 billion.

PETE
$1.9
Peterson
cashed
Blackstc
intend
substan
of the
to c

PAUL ALLEN
$775 MILLION
Soldstakes in
DreamWorks and
Oxygen Media.

GEORGE LUCAS
$200 MILLION
Sold his Hasbro
warrants at a premium.

JERRY PERENCHIO
$1.3 BILLION
In March, the TV
veteran (he was
partners with All in
the Family producer
Norman Lear) said
adios to Univision, the
nation's largest Spanish-
language broadcaster,
in exchange for
$13.7 billion.

MICHAEL KRASNY
$970 MILLION
CDW off-loaded for
$7.3 billion.

PHILIP KNIGHT
$780 MILLION
Unloaded Nike stock.

**MICKY ARISON
AND FAMILY**
$520 MILLION
Sale of Carnival stock.

HAIM SABAN
$970 MILLION
The former music
promoter earned his
first fortune with the
Mighty Morphin'
Power Rangers.
He made billion
selling a big
piece of German
broadcaster
ProSiebenSat.1
Media AG.

RAM SHRIRAM
$272 MILLION
An early backer of
Google, Shriram has
put more than three
million shares of
the Internet-search
company on the
block since it went
public, in 2005.

BARRY DILLER
$300 MILLION
All in a day's work.

CHANDLER FAMILY
$1.7 BILLION
Newspaper clan
pushed for the sale
of Tribune Co.

J. DARIUS BIKOFF
$325 MILLION
Bikoff founded
Glacéau, maker of
Vitaminwater
and Smartwater,
after finding
contaminants in his
bottled water.
Coca-Cola guzzled it
up for $4.1 billion,
likely earning him
far more than
$325 million.

ISADORE SHARP
$288 MILLION
Four Seasons
hotel chain sold
for $3.7 billion.

DWIGHT SCHAR
$193 MILLION
Sold NVR shares.

PHILLIP RUFFIN
$1.2 BILLION
Sold a 34-acre
parcel in Las Vegas
for $1.2 billion.

ROXANNE QUIMBY
$185 MILLION
Clorox bought her
eco-friendly
cosmetics concern.

ERIC SCHMIDT
$600 MILLION
Unloaded Google stock.

NICHOLAS HANAUER
$282 MILLION
Tech outfit
AQuantive bought
by Microsoft
for $6 billion.

LEWIS EISENBERG
$356 MILLION
Flipped the
switch on ITC
Holdings stock.

JOHN DOERR
$250 MILLION
The Silicon Valley
venture capitalist has
made a number of
prescient investments,
few sweeter than
Google. He still has
plenty of shares
stashed away.

Th
m
wo
re
ce
ap

MARC BENIOFF
$190 MILLION
Dispensed
Salesforce.com
stock.

RAY DAVIS
$600 MILLION
After a career in
the energy
business, the
Texan called it
quits—and then
cashed out
$600 million in
the Energy
Transfer I.P.O.

LEONARD RIGGIO
$200 MILLION
Closed the book on
GameStop shares.

SUMNER REDSTONE
$362 MILLION
Cranky Viacom
overlord sold stock.

REUBEN MARK
$230 MILLION
Former Colgate-Palmolive
chief cleansed his portfolio.

JAMES KIM AND FAMILY
$278 MILLION
Three years ago Kim
peddled his retail
chain, Electronics
Boutique, to GameStop
for $1.4 billion
in cash and stock.
He's been selling
shares ever since.

RONALD TUTOR
$182 MILLION
Perini chief sold stock.

WILLIAM POLLOCK
$183 MILLION
Online venture
Laureate Education
sold for $3.4 billion.

HAROLD HAMM
$291 MILLION
The Oklahoma
wildcatter tapped into
a billion-dollar fortune
by taking Continental
Resources, his oil-
and-gas-exploration
company, public.

RANDAL J. KIRK
$1.2 BILLION
Sold New River
Pharmaceuticals
for $2.6 billion.

BILL GATES
$2.8 BILLION
The world's richest
man sold $2.5 billion
worth of Microsoft
stock last year—
plus dividends.

ARMANDO C
$190 MILLI
His real-estate
railroad opera
bought by Fo
for $3.5 bill

STEPHEN SCHWARZMAN
$677 MILLION
Blackstone public offering.

HOW MUCH MONEY IS ALL OF THIS?

If all the dollars
identified on this page
($29,336,000,000),
were stacked, they
would reach the height
of the International
Space Station over...
NINE TIMES!
(1,990 MILES)

ORBIT

DOLLARS

EARTH
(not actual size)

SOURCE: V.F. estimates, FactSet Research Systems, Forbes   APRIL 2008   APRIL 2008   ILLUSTRATIO

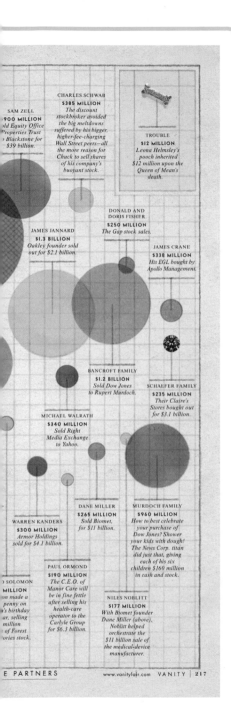

CHARLES SCHWAB
$385 MILLION
The discount stockbroker avoided the big meltdowns suffered by his bigger, higher-fee-charging Wall Street peers—all the more reason for Chuck to sell shares of his company's buoyant stock.

SAM ZELL
900 MILLION
ld Equity Office
Properties Trust
Blackstone for
$39 billion.

TROUBLE
$12 MILLION
Leona Helmsley's pooch inherited $12 million upon the Queen of Mean's death.

DONALD AND
DORIS FISHER
$250 MILLION
The Gap stock sales.

JAMES JANNARD
$1.3 BILLION
Oakley founder sold out for $2.1 billion.

JAMES CRANE
$338 MILLION
His EGL bought by Apollo Management.

BANCROFT FAMILY
$1.2 BILLION
Sold Dow Jones to Rupert Murdoch.

SCHAEFER FAMILY
$235 MILLION
Their Claire's Stores bought out for $3.1 billion.

MICHAEL WALRATH
$340 MILLION
Sold Right Media Exchange to Yahoo.

WARREN KANDERS
$300 MILLION
Armor Holdings sold for $4.1 billion.

DANE MILLER
$265 MILLION
Sold Biomet, for $11 billion.

MURDOCH FAMILY
$960 MILLION
How to best celebrate your purchase of Dow Jones? Shower your kids with dough! The News Corp. titan did just that, giving each of his six children $160 million in cash and stock.

PAUL ORMOND
$190 MILLION
The C.E.O. of Manor Care will be in fine fettle after selling his health-care operator to the Carlyle Group for $6.3 billion.

SOLOMON
MILLION
on made a
penny on
's birthday
ar, selling
million
of Forest
ories stock.

NILES NOBLITT
$177 MILLION
With Biomet founder Dane Miller (above), Noblitt helped orchestrate the $11 billion sale of the medical-device manufacturer.

E PARTNERS
www.vanityfair.com   VANITY | 217

THE 2007 WINDFALL REPORT
Design by Jason Mannix

Client: *Vanity Fair* magazine
Design firm: Doyle Partners
Art direction: Stephen Doyle

The 2007 Windfall Report featured in *Vanity Fair* magazine tells the reader, simply and amusingly, who made how much, and how. This beautifully crafted diagram uses a mix of hand-drawn and found circular items of varying scale to represent the huge sums of money made in 2007 by some of the USA's wealthiest individuals.

The largest "planet" is represented by a gold orb, belonging to Bill Gates. It represents the $2.8 billion he made by selling Microsoft stock options, plus dividends, in 2007. To contrast with this, one of the smallest "stars" of this Vanity Fair firmament belongs to Niles Noblitt—it illustrates the mere $177 million he made when he helped to orchestrate the sale of medical device manufacturer Biomet.

reference

This apparently random group of circular shapes is reminiscent of historic planetary charts, with each "planet" or "star" being shown to represent the annual earnings of a member of the financial elite. Annotations are used to explain how much money has been made, with the hand-drawn feel used to reinforce a sense of history, quality, and prestige.

TRENDS IN RELATIVE SEA LEVEL
IN VENICE
Design by Joel Katz

Client: Albert Ammerman
Design firm: Joel Katz Design Associates
Art direction: Joel Katz

Over the last 2,000 years the sea level in the Venetian lagoon has risen dramatically. Archaeologist Albert Ammerman has taken core drillings for analysis and some of the results of this research are visualized in this chart. Designer Joel Katz says, "Multiple categories of information make this design extremely complex. The form realizes the information, and as the information within the graph increases in multivariancy, it becomes more difficult and more important to show the data and the relationship between data categories with clarity and simplicity."

TRENDS IN RELATIVE SEA LEVEL IN
BASED ON ARCHAEOLOGICAL EVIDENCE
SECOND APPROXIMATION 2003

ELEVATIONS
TO THE
1897 STANDARD
METERS

+1.5

+1.0

+0.5

1897-0

-0.5

-1.0

-1.5

-2.0

-2.5

LEGEND

Dates of construction

Artifact code L4 Level of artifact

L4 Presumed mean sea level

T6

T7

T9 T8

D4

D5

D6

T10

D7

AD 200 400

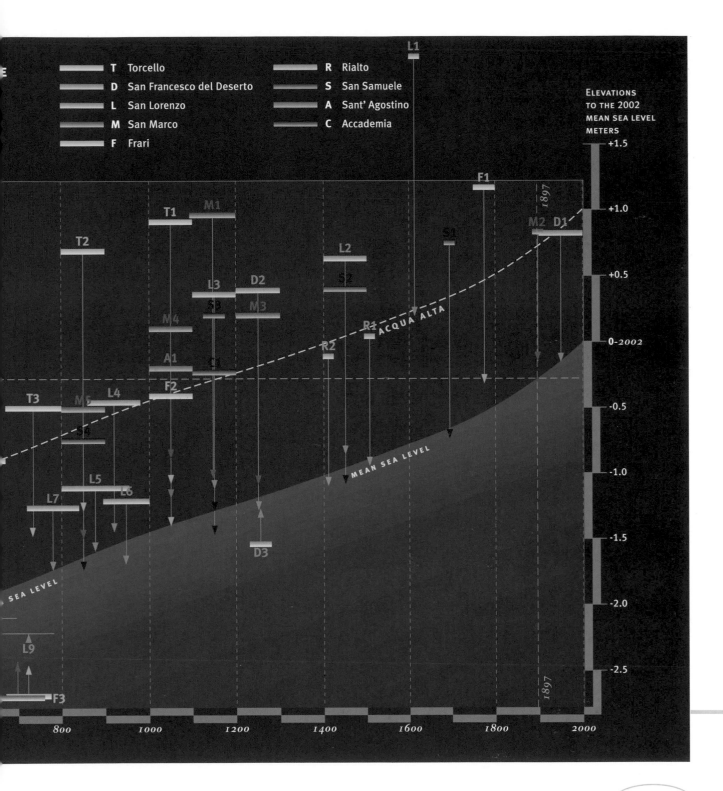

T Torcello
D San Francesco del Deserto
L San Lorenzo
M San Marco
F Frari

R Rialto
S San Samuele
A Sant' Agostino
C Accademia

ELEVATIONS
TO THE 2002
MEAN SEA LEVEL
METERS

+1.5
+1.0
+0.5
0-2002
-0.5
-1.0
-1.5
-2.0
-2.5

L1
F1
M2 D1
S1
T1 M1
T2
L2
L3 D2
S2
M4 S3 M3
R1
A1 C1
R2
T3 M5 L4
F2
S4
L5
L7 L6
ACQUA ALTA
MEAN SEA LEVEL
SEA LEVEL
1897
1897
D3
L9
F3

800   1000   1200   1400   1600   1800   2000

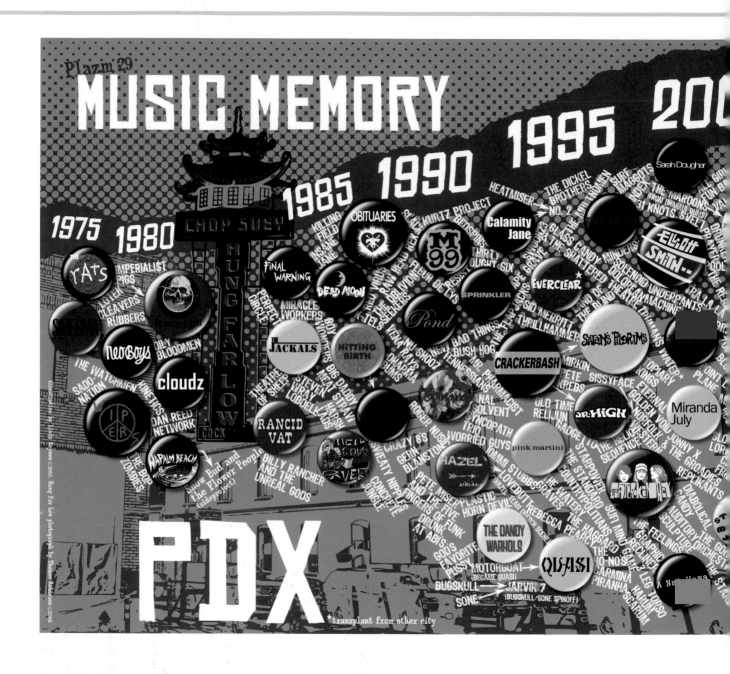

PDX MUSIC MEMORY
Design by Linda Reynen

Client: Plazm #29
Design firm: Plazm
Art direction: Joshua Berger

Plazm designed a pullout poster to chart and document the history of the independent music scene in Portland, Oregon, USA. A mix of all-caps listings of bands and images of brightly colored promotional buttons, spanning the period between 1975 and 2005, charts the remarkable growth and increase in popularity of this music scene.

reference

The chart clearly draws its inspiration from a number of artistic and cultural movements, including the pop art creations of the 1960s, and the punk style that Malcolm McLaren and Vivien Westwood made popular in the 1970s. High-contrast imagery and enlarged dot screens are seen in many well-known pop-art pieces, including the works of Andy Warhol and Roy Lichtenstein. Ripped edges, garish color, and a general nonconformist approach to design and typography are familiar design features of punk fashion and the music scene of 1970s London.

MOVE OUR MONEY
Design by Stefan Sagmeister
and Hjalti Karlsson

Client: Business Leaders for
Sensible Priorities
Design firm: Stefan Sagmeister
Art direction: Stefan Sagmeister

Move Our Money was an initiative devised
by Ben Cohen of Ben & Jerry's fame. The
idea behind this campaign was to cut
the US military budget and move the
money saved to spending on education
and health. Instead of a formal logo,
Sagmeister designed simplified graphs
to illustrate the level of military spending.

Some of these charts were designed as
huge, inflatable sculptures that could be
taken around the US as part of a movable
road show; others were composed of
stacks of huge cookies piled up to various
levels to indicate spending differentials.

Sagmeister also designed a simple
pullout graph for incorporation into
a pen, as an everyday reminder of the
disparity in government spending.

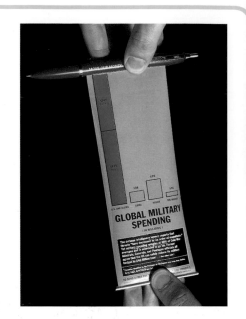

The inspiration behind these pieces comes from childhood favorites, namely cookies and inflatable toys, both of which provide a simple and effective alternative to the conventional bar chart.

ALERT-O-MAT
Design by Stephen Doyle

Client: *The New York Times*
Design firm: Doyle Partners
Art direction: Stephen Doyle

This design by Doyle Partners is a diagrammatic, color-coded alert hoax that was used to illustrate an article concerning the post-9/11 concerns in the USA. Fourteen states of anxiety are listed in the colorful sections of the "Alert-o-mat official wheel of risk."

reference

The inspiration behind the Alert-o-mat was the popular family game Twister by MB games. Twister contains a spinning arrow that is used to provide random instructions to players of the game, for example place your left hand on a blue spot and your right foot on a red spot, in much the same way as random "instructions" are provided by the Alert-o-mat.

DIAGRAMS: Innovative Solutions for Graphic Designers

4 REASONS WHY YOU SHOULD VOTE
Design by Katie Mangano

Client: AIGA Get out the Vote 2008
Design firm: MSLK
Art direction: Marc S. Levitt
  and Sheri L. Koetting
Typography: Katie Mangano

This poster uses humorous statistics to encourage the 18–25 demographic to participate in the US national elections of fall 2008. The data featured in these charts is fabricated so that the information graphics double as typographic forms that spell out the word "vote." Designer Katie Mangano explains, "We wanted to mimic the statistics typically seen during an election year in a way that would attract young voters' attention and be amusing. In the end, we provided four unusually compelling reasons to vote."

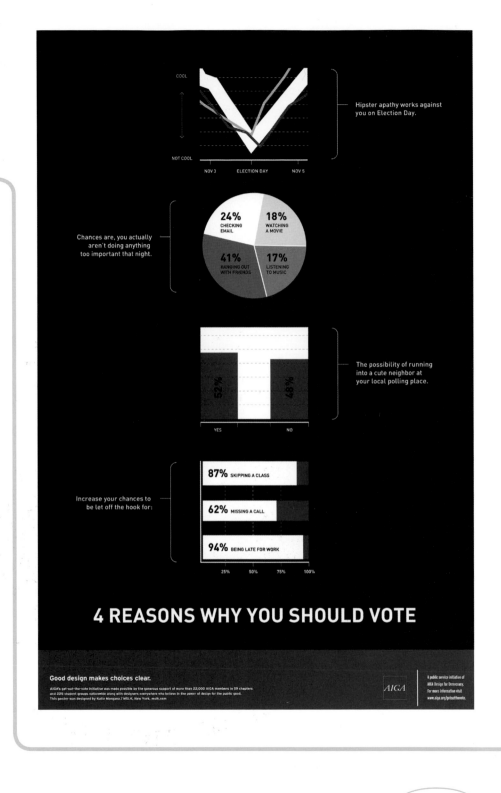

PATTERNS IN OSCAR-WINNING MOVIES
Design by Pitch Interactive, Ltd.

Client: Self-initiated
Design firm: Pitch Interactive, Ltd.
Art direction: Wesley Grubbs
Programming: Nick Yahnke

This image charts the relationships between directors, Oscar-winning actors, non-Oscar-winning actors, and Oscar-winning movies from 2000 to 2006. Pattern is the first thing the reader sees on viewing this fascinating diagram, and then the complex detail comes into view. Three circular paths differentiate directors (listed around the central circle) from Oscar-winning actors (listed around the second circle), and non-Oscar-winning actors (listed around the outer circle). Curved lines plot the relationships between directors and Oscar-winning actors, and between Oscar-winning actors and non-Oscar-winning actors. Each line

is semitransparent so that when multiple relationships occur between individuals, the color intensity of the line increases. While the names of the directors and Oscar-winning actors can be difficult to read, specific patterns in the relationships can clearly be seen. For example, the chart reveals that very few non-Oscar-winning actors have worked with multiple Oscar-winning actors more than once.

As designer Wesley Grubbs explains, the design team didn't know what they were going to come up with. Ultimately, they wanted to show something simple, yet retain the complexity of the data.

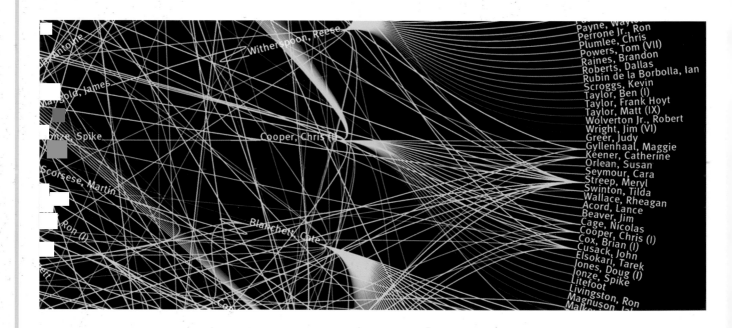

L'ELLIPSE
Design by Adrienne Bornstein

Client: Self-initiated
Design firm: Bornstein & Sponchiado
Art direction: Adrienne Bornstein
Illustration: Adrienne Bornstein
Photography: Adrienne Bornstein

L'Ellipse is a special issue of a magazine dedicated to extraterrestrial phenomena. This piece illustrates the earth landing of an extraterrestrial hen, from the planet Houlette. It includes a diagrammatic interpretation of a group of buildings. Each building is shown in perspective, but without architectural detail such as windows and doors. A network of paths, roadways, and underground communication links connects each property, and a grayscale image of a building gives the reader a mental picture of the property.

Adrienne Bornstein selected a limited color palette, using only red and black plus shades of gray. Red is used to highlight areas that have a direct connection with the extra-terrestrial experience; black is used to hold other diagrammatic detail and type.

One diagram shows the position of Houlette in the context of the solar system and indicates the chicken's route to earth, while another compares a real chicken's skeleton with its extraterrestrial counterpart.

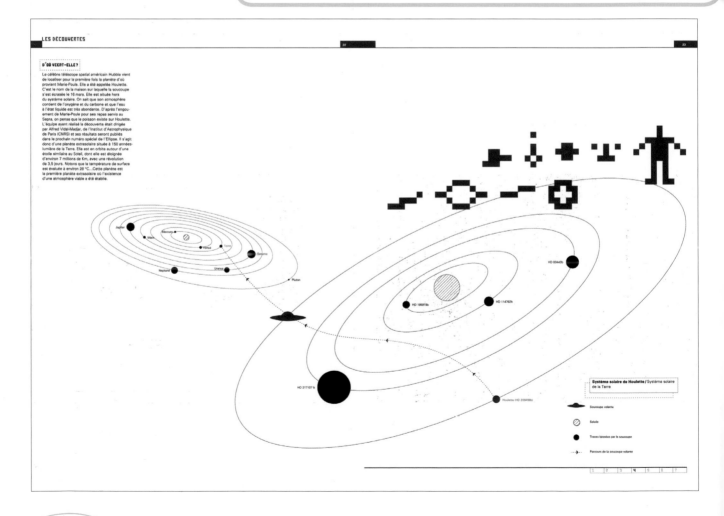

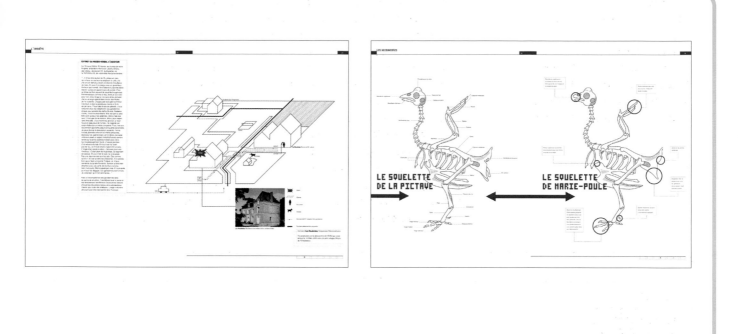

LE SQUELETTE DE LA PICTAVE ← → LE SQUELETTE DE MARIE-POULE

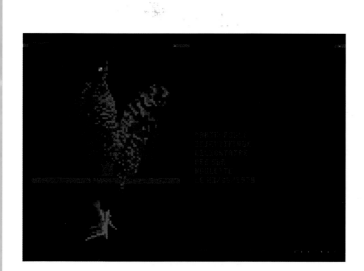

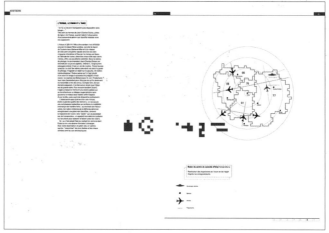

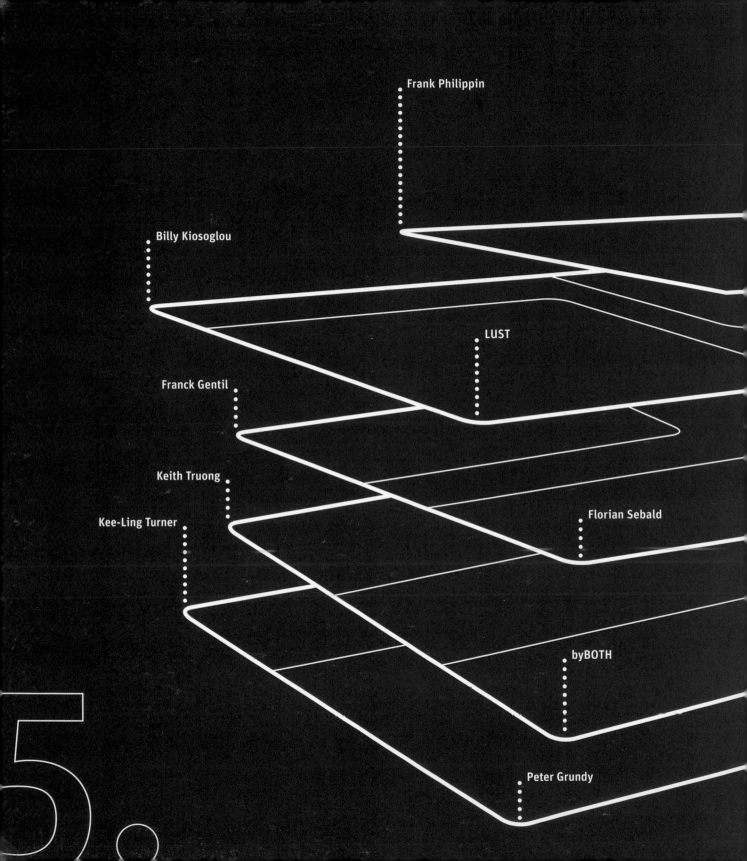

Frank Philippin

Billy Kiosoglou

LUST

Franck Gentil

Keith Truong

Kee-Ling Turner

Florian Sebald

byBOTH

Peter Grundy

5.

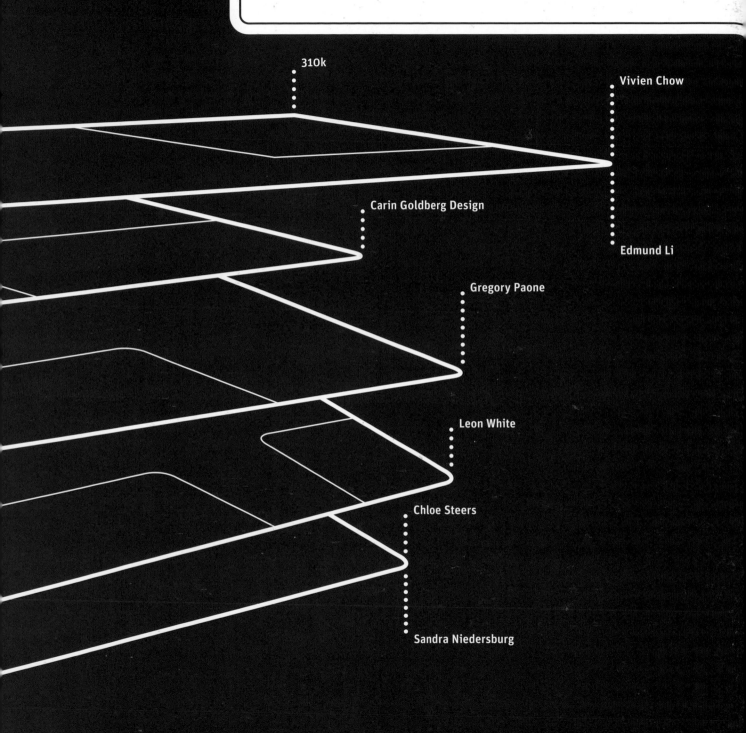

310k

Vivien Chow

Carin Goldberg Design

Edmund Li

Gregory Paone

Leon White

Chloe Steers

Sandra Niedersburg

THIRTIETH ANNIVERSARY
INVITATION POSTERS
**Design by Frank Philippin
and Billy Kiosoglou**

Client: Thurm & Dinges
Design firm: Brighten the Corners
Art direction: Frank Philippin
　　and Billy Kiosoglou
Typography: Frank Philippin
　　and Billy Kiosoglou
Illustration: Frank Philippin

Many diagrams represent a process.
In this case it is the passing of time—
30 years to be exact—since the
establishment of Thurm & Dinges.
Brighten the Corners' solution was to
show the passing of time typographically,
using a blend of outline sans-serif
numerals to take the viewer through
the visual transformation of the date
from 1971 to 2001.

Inspiration was drawn from blueprint diagrams used by the engineering company Thurm & Dinges. These gave Frank Philippin and Billy Kiosoglou the idea of using outline letterforms, and also of using cyan as a single color.

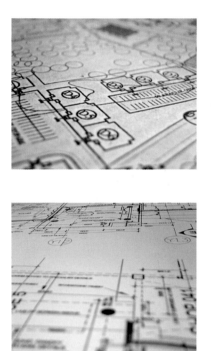

1971 – 2001

Thurm & Dinges Planungsgesellschaft mbh

BATTLE OF TRAFALGAR POSTAGE STAMPS
Design by Peter Grundy

Client: Royal Mail
Design firm: Grundini Ltd.
Illustration: Peter Grundy

Each tiny stamp in this Battle of Trafalgar series is used to convey a wealth of fascinating information. The 40-pence stamp gives information about a sailor's typical meal, and the 43-pence stamp shows a height and length comparison of HMS *Victory*; a London bus; Nelson's column in Trafalgar Square, London; and the Royal Navy submarine, HMS *Dreadnought*. The 47- and 57-pence stamps carry diagrammatic interpretations of surprising historical facts.

The miniature diagram on the 47-pence stamp pinpoints the location of the battle through a simplified image of the Spanish coast, a precise indication of scale (in miles), and an orientation to north. The final stamp in the series informs the reader that HMS *Victory*'s 820-man crew came from 18 far-flung countries.

reference

The facts surrounding the Battle of Trafalgar were the inspiration behind this unpublished series, designed by Peter Grundy for the UK's Royal Mail.

NEW YEAR'S PARTY INVITATION
Design by Carin Goldberg Design

Client: Self-initiated
Design firm: Carin Goldberg Design
Art direction: Carin Goldberg Design
Typography: Carin Goldberg Design
Illustration: Carin Goldberg Design

Carin Goldberg used a selection of scattered Pantone chips to denote significant features of the New Year's party she threw with James Biber; her distinctive handwriting and annotation direct the reader from one element to another. Pantone chip 1495 C is used to symbolize carrots, provide subway details, and, by means of a lengthy arrow, to lead the reader to the statement "Fun in Brooklyn." Pantone chip 7541 C is used to symbolize white couches, dip, and the color of Lily the dog, leaving the reader to imagine the real-life connection between the three.

reference

Carin's inspiration for this design was a random collection of scattered Pantone chips that reminded her of the confetti often used at celebrations.

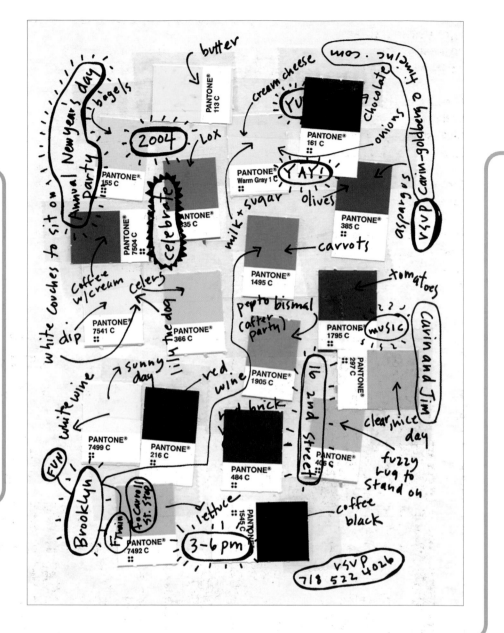

LEARN GERMAN WORLD CUP POSTCARDS
Design by Frank Philippin and Billy Kiosoglou

Client: Goethe-Institut London and DAAD London (Deutscher Akademischer Austausch Dienst/ German Academic Exchange Service)
Design firm: Brighten the Corners
Art direction: Frank Philippin and Billy Kiosoglou
Typography: Frank Philippin and Billy Kiosoglou

Communicating information about "how England can win the football World Cup 2006" within the context of learning a new language—German—was the main purpose of these postcards. The 12 cards, each devoted to one England player, feature a diagram that illustrates how that particular player can either score a goal, or contribute to the scoring of a goal, and, of course, boost the chances of an English World Cup win.

reference

Frank Philippin's inspiration for this design was "the fact that the English, before every major tournament, always think that they can win it. The postcards explore that statement in an ironic way and say, 'of course, this is much easier said than done.'"

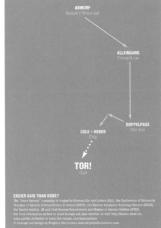

AGDA NATIONAL AWARDS EXHIBITION
Design by Franck Gentil and Keith Truong

Client: Australian Graphic Design Association
Design firm: Beam
Typography: Kee-Ling Turner
Illustration: Sarah Lincoln
Photography: Anthony Geernaert

More than simply "how-to assemble" guides, these graphic representations by Beam Design are also event promotions, enticing the prospective audience to come along and experience a stunning, specially created, contemporary environment.

reference

Commenting on the inspiration behind this piece, Franck Gentil says, "The diagram's design is similar to IKEA's single-color flatpack instructions. It is rooted in the style of the thumbnail visuals produced to underpin this project."

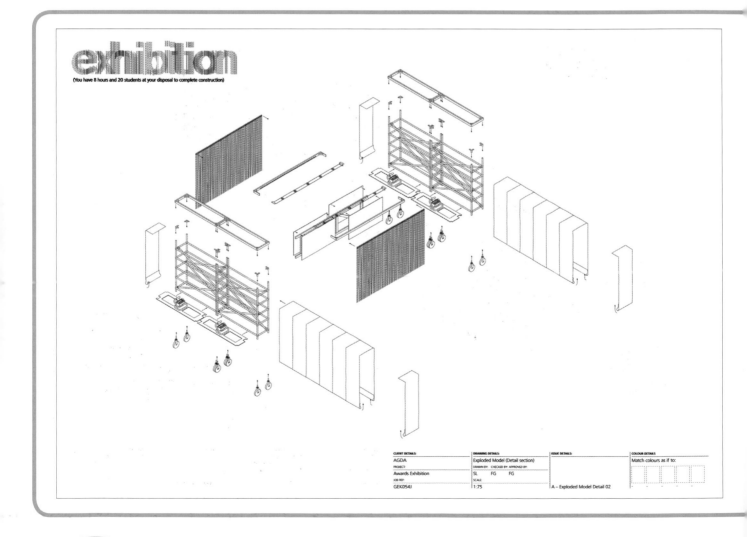

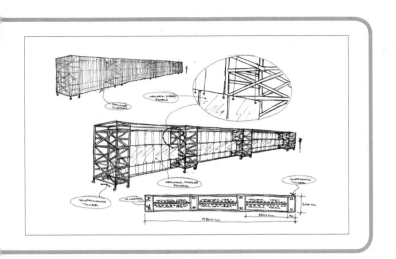

exhibition

(You have 8 hours and 20 students at your disposal to complete construction)

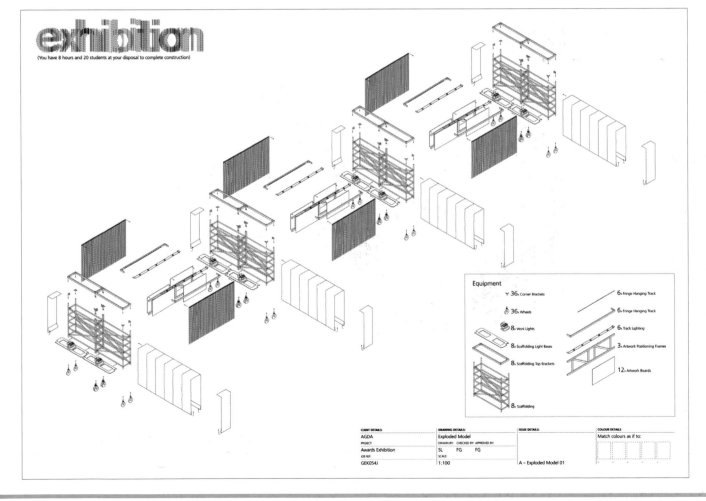

Equipment

36x Corner Brackets	6x Fringe Hanging Track
36x Wheels	6x Fringe Hanging Track
8x Work Lights	6x Track Lighting
8x Scaffolding Light Bases	3x Artwork Positioning Frames
8x Scaffolding Top Brackets	12x Artwork Boards
8x Scaffolding	

CLIENT DETAILS:	DRAWING DETAILS:	ISSUE DETAILS:	COLOUR DETAILS
AGDA	Exploded Model		Match colours as if to:
PROJECT	DRAWN BY: CHECKED BY: APPROVED BY:		
Awards Exhibition	SL FG FG		
JOB REF:	SCALE:		
GEK054J	1:100	A – Exploded Model 01	

SYDNEY TOWER
Design by Franck Gentil and
Kee-Ling Turner

Clients: Sydney Attractions Group
and Westfield
Design firm: Beam
Art direction: Franck Gentil
Typography: Kee-Ling Turner
Photography: Adrian Lander

Sydney Tower is a popular visitor destination in Sydney, Australia. The construction of the tower began in 1970, and by 1972, 52 stores in the tower had opened. In 1974, the office element of this project was completed and finally, in 1981, the tower opened to the public as a visitor attraction. The structure is one of the safest high-tower buildings in the world; it uses 56 stabilizing cables to ensure that the building will withstand rough weather conditions and earthquakes.

The main objective of these diagrams is to build visitor anticipation while providing clear information about the tower. Each panel has a striking visual presence; blocks of statistical information are complemented by monochromatic background illustrations that tell the story of this iconic structure.

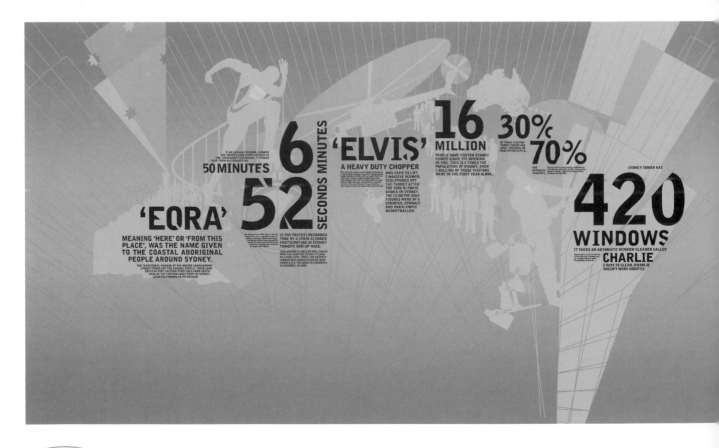

DIAGRAMS: Innovative Solutions for Graphic Designers

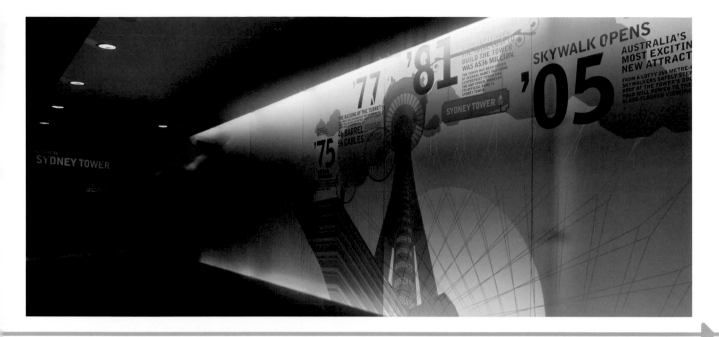

The tower and its distinctive cabling were the strongest influence behind Beam's design for the diagrammatic panels displayed in the visitor center. Within each panel, the subtle cables create a sunbeam effect. The treatment of this design element was influenced by the sunburst designs and high-contrast illustration style popular during the art-deco period.

THE TOTAL WEIGHT OF THE TOWER (SHAFT & TURRET) IS 4067 TONNES – THE SAME AS

4 MANLY FERRIES

10 JUMBO JETS

37 BLUE WHALES

IT IS 2395 KILOMETRES FROM LONDON TO ATHENS OR MELBOURNE TO CAIRNS. IF THE WIRES IN THE TOWER'S SECURING CABLES WERE LAID END TO END, THEY WOULD COVER THE SAME DISTANCE.

THE LARGEST LIVING AUSTRALIAN TREE IS A MOUNTAIN ASH, KNOWN AS

'007'

(EUCALYPTUS REGNANS)

2 MORE TOP COATS

885

SMITHSONIAN HALL OF MAMMALS
Design by Edmund Li

Client: Smithsonian Institute
Design firm: Reich + Petch
Principal: Tony Reich
Photography: Kerun Ip
Exhibition director: Stephen Petri
Exhibition design: Fang-Pin Lee and
  Pauline Dolovich
Copywriting: Sharon Barry

This diagram, which is part of a 3D display within the Smithsonian Mammals exhibition, explains the concept that all mammals are linked to a common ancestor that existed 210 million years ago. "This is a difficult, but important concept that the museum hopes to deliver to visitors to the exhibit. With the high number of visitors—millions each year—and the fact that each person, on average, spends less than 15 minutes at each display, the design has to be simple in order to get the message across efficiently," says Tony Reich.

reference

Inspiration for this design approach came from the huge diversity of shape and form that mammals possess: from four legs to two, from long necks to short, and from antlers and horns to tails and fins. Reich + Petch have created silhouettes that reflect the stance and movement of individual mammals: jaguars run across the page, while kangaroos hop, and the human figure appears to be on the brink of jumping for joy.

From one ancestor, many mammals

WEST WALL

SOUTH WALL

EAST WALL

NORTH WALL

PAONE SCHARF WEDDING INVITATION
Design by Gregory Paone

Client: Elizabeth Paone
and Michael Scharf
Design firm: Paone Design Associates
Art direction: Gregory Paone

Gregory Paone made subtle use of color in the map that accompanied his sister's wedding invitation, but the most striking element of this piece is the simplification of the road system. The alternative routes around the one-way system from the church to the reception hotel are indicated using fine pink lines—one solid and one dotted.

The street network is indicated as a fine white mesh of lines, with inspiration coming from the grid systems visible in plaid fabric.

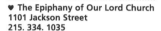

♥ **The Epiphany of Our Lord Church**
1101 Jackson Street
215. 334. 1035
From Hotel Parking Lot : Turn right onto 36th Street to Market Street, one block. Turn right on Market to 15th Street, twenty-one blocks. Turn right on 15th and bear right. Follow 15th to Locust Street, four blocks. Turn left on Locust to 10th Street, five blocks. Turn right on 10th to Jackson Street, twenty-two blocks. Turn right on Jackson to Epiphany Parking Lot Entrance between 11th and 12th Streets.

★ **Sheraton University City Hotel**
36th and Chestnut Streets
215. 387. 8000
From Church Parking Lot : Turn right onto Jackson Street to 13th Street, one block. Turn right on 13th to Snyder Avenue, one block. Turn right on Snyder to 11th Street, two blocks. Turn left on 11th to Walnut Street, twenty-two blocks. Turn left on Walnut to 36th Street, twenty-five blocks. Turn right on 36th to Sheraton Parking Lot Entrance just North of Chestnut Street.

UNITED NATIONS OF LOVE
Design by Florian Sebald

Client: Bpitchcontrol.de
Design firm: Pfadfinderei

Berlin-based music label Bpitchcontrol commissioned Pfadfinderei to produce designs for a commemorative T-shirt for Berlin's annual Love Parade. This street parade is a festival of music and dance to celebrate Berlin's reunification.

Pfadfinderei chose this diagrammatic solution for its aesthetic appeal rather than its informative qualities.

The back of the T-shirt features a world map composed of hearts rotated to interlock and form recognizable land masses, with color used to indicate different countries and states.

reference

This map was inspired by the designs of the 1960s and 1970s. The heart was one of the most famous icons of this time, with a particularly popular and widely acclaimed example being Milton Glaser's much-reproduced logo "I ❤ NY."

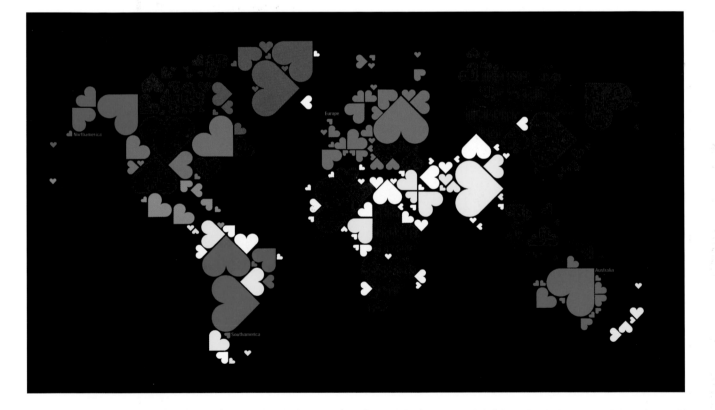

URBAN EXPLORERS FESTIVAL
Design by 31Ok

Client: CBK Doordrecht, Urban
   Explorers Festival
Design firm: 31Ok
Art direction: 31Ok
Typography: 31Ok
Illustration: 31Ok

31Ok created a character, UE, to help guide visitors around the city of Amsterdam, and to find every element of the various events of the Urban Explorers Festival. The examples featured here show UE at various festival locations, with diagrammatic notation indicating venue layouts. A selection of computer keyboard strokes is grouped to give an indication of the events and environments to be enjoyed by the festival attendee.

reference

31Ok cite urban street art, gallery art, music events, and city fun as the inspiration behind these diagrams, but undoubtedly, the graphics of early computer games have also been a strong influence.

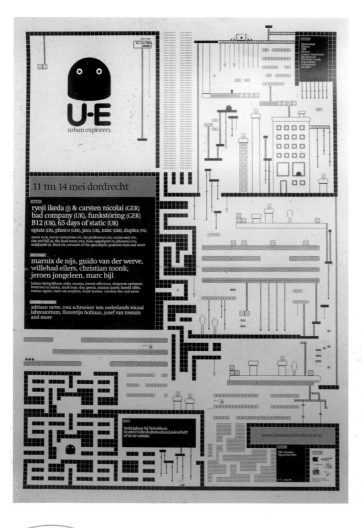

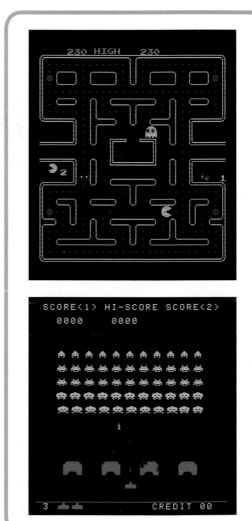

AT RANDOM? NETWORKS AND CROSS-POLLINATION
Design by LUST

Client: Museum De Pavilijoens, Almere
Design firm: LUST
Art direction: LUST

Surely one of the great pleasures for any graphic designer, and certainly the inspiration behind this design, is the act of running fingers over stacks of paper and admiring the beauty of piles of same-sized sheets, laid one on top of the other.

This project involves the creation of unique exhibition catalogs, printed individually on demand, using a copier and different-colored paper. The environment within which the copier and catalog paper is located plays an important element in the design. LUST's presentation of this piece, with colored paper in precise, tidy piles against a bright white wall, provides the reader with an instant 3D graph that accurately reflects the popularity of one colorway over another. The statistics are the result of each individual's interaction with this project.

I AM A CURATOR
Design by byBOTH

Clients: Per Hüttner and the
Chisenhale Gallery
Design firm: byBOTH

This design features mainly text-based
and statistical material. Every day, for
30 days, an independent visitor entered
the gallery and curated their own private
exhibition, sourced from a supplied
archive of art. Their experience provided
the data recorded in the catalog.

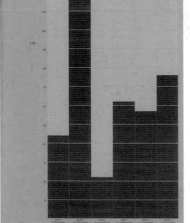

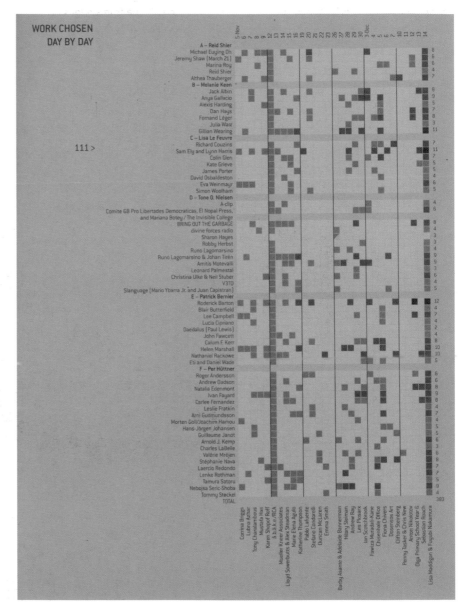

byBOTH explains, "We saw the opportunity to extend our role as pure designers and take a more active part in the creation of content. During our initial meetings with Per, he mentioned an interest in the potential of 'graphing' some of the data that had been collected, and we saw this as a perfect opportunity to create fluxions in the flow of the book.

About halfway through, we realized we were creating a table of comparison between the visiting curators."

byBoth used the very subtle color contrast created by printing two Pantone inks on light gray, uncoated stock to indicate the frame edges of both charts and graphs. Each table is simply designed using small circular or square shapes to record the use of individual items of art. The resulting set of graphs provides the reader with an instant indication of the popularity of specific works during the six weeks of the exhibition.

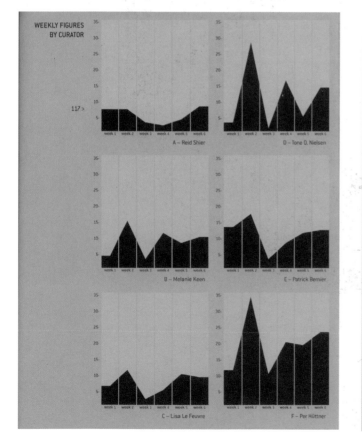

WEEKLY FIGURES BY CURATOR

117 >

A – Reid Shier

D – Tone O. Nielsen

B – Melanie Keen

E – Patrick Bernier

C – Lisa Le Feuvre

F – Per Hüttner

WORK CHOSEN

113 >

A – Reid Shier

Michael Euying Oh	8
Jeremy Shaw (March 21)	6
Marina Roy	6
Reid Shier	4
Althea Thauberger	7

B – Melanie Keen

Jack Albin	8
Anya Gallacio	9
Alexis Harding	5
Dan Hays	7
Fernand Léger	8
Julia Warr	3
Gillian Wearing	11

C – Lisa Le Feuvre

Richard Couzins	7
Sam Ely and Lynn Harris	11
Colin Glen	7
Kate Grieve	5
James Porter	5
David Osbaldeston	4
Eva Weinmayr	4
Simon Woolham	5

D – Tone O. Nielsen

A-clip	4
Comité 68 Pro Libertades Democráticas, El Nopal Press, and Mariana Botey / The Invisible College	6
BRING OUT THE GARBAGE	8
divine forces radio	1/2
Sharon Hayes	
Robby Herbst	3
Runo Lagomarsino	4
Runo Lagomarsino & Johan Tiren	9
Amitis Motevalli	9
Leonard Palmestal	3
Christina Ulke & Neil Stuber	6
V310	
Slanguage (Mario Ybarra Jr. and Juan Capistran)	5

E – Patrick Bernier

Roderick Barton	12
Blair Butterfield	4
Lee Campbell	7
Lucia Cipriano	
Daedalus (Paul Lewis)	
John Fawcett	4
Calum F. Kerr	
Helen Marshall	10
Nathaniel Rackowe	10
Eti and Daniel Wade	5

F – Per Hüttner

Roger Andersson	6
Andrew Dadson	5
Natalia Edenmont	8
Ivan Fayard	9
Carlee Fernandez	8
Leslie Fratkin	4
Arni Gudmundsson	7
Morten Goll/Joachim Hamou	
Hans-Jörgen Johansen	5
Guillaume Janot	
Arnold J. Kemp	6
Charles LaBelle	
Valérie Mréjen	
Stéphanie Nava	6
Laercio Redondo	8
Lenke Rothman	7
Tamura Satoru	
Nebojsa Seric-Shoba	9
Tommy Steckel	4
TOTAL	383

SAINSBURY CENTRE FOR VISUAL ARTS: MAP, INTERPRETATION, AND SIGNAGE
Design by Sandra Niedersburg, Leon White, and Chloe Steers

Client: Sainsbury Centre For Visual Arts
Design firm: Steers McGillan Design Ltd.
Art direction: Richard McGillan

SteersMcGillan created integrated marketing, navigation, and interpretation communications for Sir Norman Foster's refurbished gallery at the Sainsbury Centre for Visual Arts at the University of East Anglia, Norwich, UK. Integrating all three elements reduced signage by 50% and helped to keep the building clutter-free, but well branded.

Each element within the design has a strong visual association, based on the use of image, color, typography, and groupings, to name just a few factors. The map shown here uses light shades of gray set against a background of dark gray. The floor plans are layered, in perspective, and annotated.

reference

The inspiration behind this design was the modernist architecture of the Sainsbury building itself, opened in the 1970s and designed by the internationally renowned architect Sir Norman Foster.

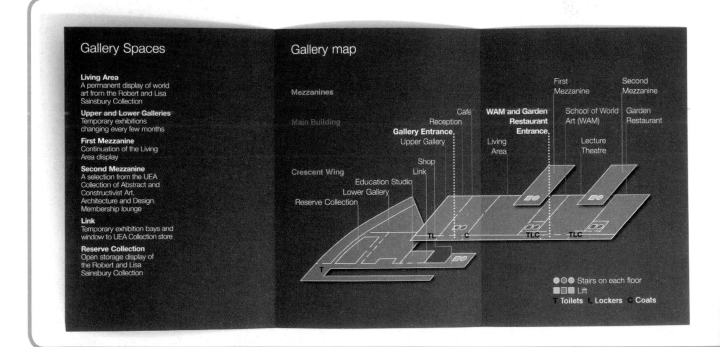

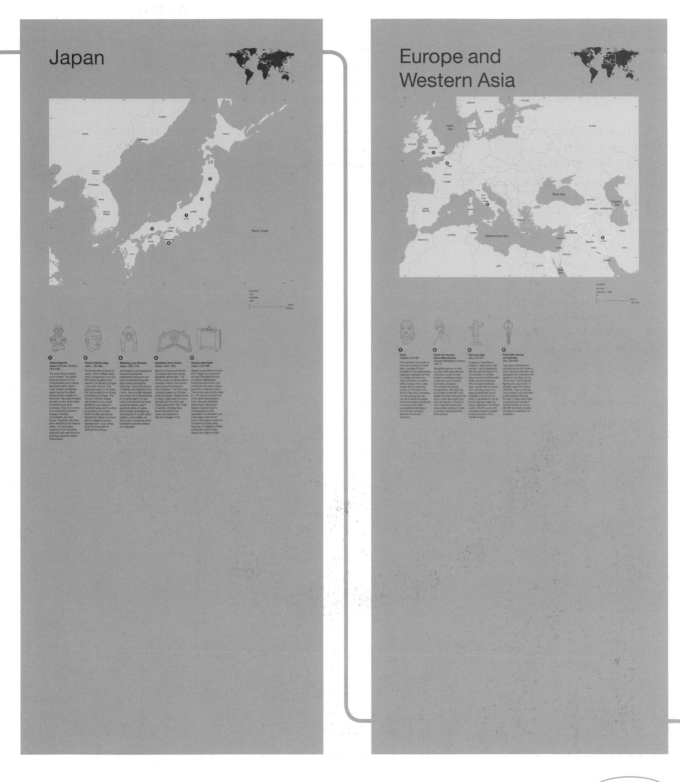

BUTTERFLIES AND PLANTS:
PARTNERS IN EVOLUTION
Design by Edmund Li and Vivien Chow

Client: Smithsonian Institution
Design firm: Reich + Petch
Art direction: Edmund Li
Principal in charge: Tony Reich
Illustration: Mary Parrish and
  Emily Damstra
Photography: Jiri VonDrak
Exhibition director: Stephen Petri
Exhibition design: Fang-Pin Lee
  and Pauline Dolovich

The Butterflies and Plants: Partners in Evolution exhibition explains the coevolution of butterflies and plants. This complex, multifaceted design project includes icons, information panels, and a floor plan of the Smithsonian Pavilion. The floor plan is drawn in perspective, and locates the building within its block of streets and in relation to the butterfly garden. Color is used to highlight pertinent areas, with shades of yellow, blue, and green selected because they feature within the exhibition display panels, diagrams, and graphs.

The floor plan is displayed prominently at entrance points to the exhibition, set within a distinctively shaped panel. This shape is a constant feature in the exhibition, used to frame diagrams, graphs, and illustrations. The slight angling of the panel sides echoes the shape of butterfly wings.

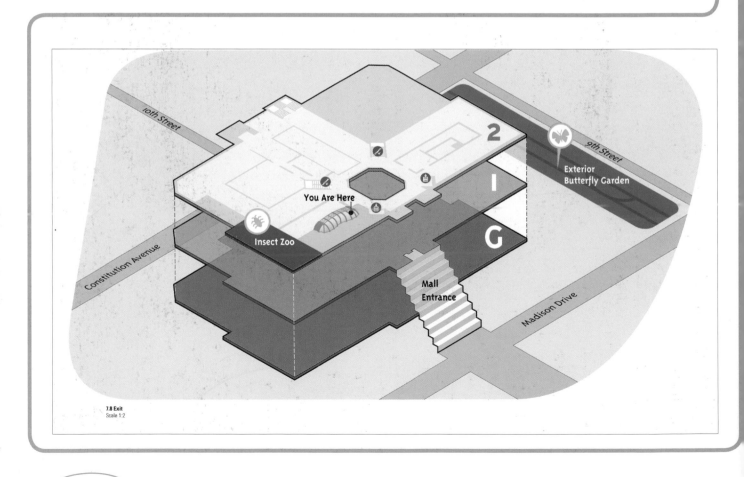

"The inspiration behind these designs comes from the color and form of the subject matter. Although specimens tend to be tiny, we have used oversized imagery to create a dramatic contrast. Brilliant color and butterfly-inspired 'graphic carriers' help convey the important messages of the exhibition, and ensure that the specimens and facts have the attention they deserve," explains Edmund Li of Reich + Petch.

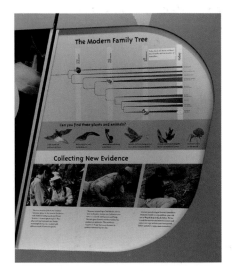

Directory

310k
Jan Hanzenstraat 78hs
Amsterdam 1053 ST
The Netherlands
me@310k.nl

the apartment
101 Crosby St
New York City
NY 10012
USA
hello@welcometomeet.com

ArthurSteenHorneAdamson
404 Eagle Tower
Montpellier Dr
Cheltenham
Gloucestershire GL50 1TA
UK
joe@ashaemail.co.uk

BankerWessel
Skeppsbron 10
111 30 Stockholm
Sweden
info@bankerwessel.com

Beam
Level 1, 46 Foster St
Surry Hills
Sydney
NSW 2010
Australia
franck@beamcreative.com

Eelco van den Berg
Rotterdam 3039 HE
The Netherlands
eelco@eelcovandenberg.com

boing!
Comber House
Comber Road
Kinver
Staffordshire DY7 6HT
UK

Chris Bolton
ISO Roobertinkatu 10 A 1
Helsinki 00120
Finland
chris@chrisbolton.org

Bornstein & Sponchiado
58 Rue de La Rochefoucauld
Paris 75009
France
contact@bornstein-sponchiado.com

Brighten the Corners
Unit 243, The Bon Marché Centre
241–251 Ferndale Rd
London SW9 8BJ
UK
contact@brightenthecorners.com

Browns
5 Plantain Pl
Crosby Row
London SE1 1YN
UK
nick@brownsdesign.com

byBOTH
17 Cyntra Pl
201 Mare St
London E8 3QE
UK
us@byboth.com

Carin Goldberg Design
Suite 309, 416 West 13th St
New York City
NY 10014
USA
carin@caringoldberg.com

Andrés Celesia
1032 Madero St
San Fernando
Buenos Aires 1646
Argentina
andrescelesia@hotmail.com

Coley Porter Bell
18 Grosvenor Gdns
London SW1W 0DH
UK
ridhisain@hotmail.com

Dextro.org
59 Postfach
Baden 2500
Austria
dextro@dextro.org

Doyle Partners
Suite 600, 1123 Broadway
New York
NY 10010
USA
turk@doylepartners.com

emerystudio
80 Market St
Southbank, Melbourne
Vic 3006
Australia
nicole.farquhar@emerystudio.com

Marcos Farina
marquitosfarina@gmail.com

Form
47 Tabernacle St
London EC2A 4AA
UK
studio@form.uk.com

Sebastian Gagin
Apt. 10°B, 2358 Av Ricardo Balbin
Buenos Aires C1428CVN
Argentina
sgagin@gmail.com

Lorenzo Geiger
31 Kasernenstr
Bern 3013
Switzerland
hello@lorenzogeiger.ch

Matias Gigliotti
2671 Ohiggins St
Capital Federal
Buenos Aires 1428
Argentina
matgigliotti@gmail.com

Grade Design
5 Maltings Place
169 Tower Bridge Rd
London SE1 3NA
UK
info@gradedesign.com

Greteman Group
2nd Floor, 1425 East Douglas
Wichita
KS 67211
USA
info@gretemangroup.com

Grundini Ltd.
Studio 69, 1 Town Meadow
Brentford
Middlesex TW8 0BQ
UK
peter@grundini.com

Joel Katz Design Associates
Suite 1411, 1616 Walnut St
Philadelphia
PA 19103
USA
jkatz@joelkatzdesign.com

Supriya Kalidas,
Apt. 6, 410 Pierce St
San Francisco
CA 94117
USA
supriyakalidas@gmail.com

Tae Koo
1-601 Hyundai 3 Apt.
KaePo-Dong, KangNam-Gu
Seoul 135-242
Republic of Korea
tae.koo@gmail.com

Frida Larios
21 Avenida Los Laureles
Colonia la Sultana
Antiguo Cuscatlán, La Libertad 0001
El Salvador
frida@fridalarios.com

**Louise Carrier Graphic Design
and Illustration**
26 Elliotts Lane
Codsall
South Staffordshire
West Midlands WV8 1PG
UK
louise@louisecarrier.co.uk

LUST
17 Dunne Bierkade
The Hague 2512 BC
The Netherlands
lust@lust.nl

The Luxury of Protest
82 Brune House
Bell Lane
London E1 7NP
UK
info@theluxuryofprotest.com

Arias Luz
2671 Ohiggins St
Capital Federal
Buenos Aires 1428
Argentina
ariasluz@yahoo.com.ar

MAKI
Meeuwerderweg 59
Groningen 9724 EN
The Netherlands
info@makimaki.nl

Thomas Matthews
8 Disney St
London SE1 1JF
UK
studio@thomasmatthews.com

MSLK
23–23 33rd Rd
Long Island City
NY 11106
USA
mslk@mslk.com

Muller
Unit 307, Studio 28
28 Lawrence Rd
London N15 4EG
UK
tomm@hellomuller.com

No Office
4 Witte de Withstraat
Amsterdam 1057 X
The Netherlands
info@no-office.nl

---

notNeutral
Suite 101, 639 North Larchmont Blvd
Los Angeles
CA 90004
USA
julie@notneutral.com

Paone Design Associates
240 South 20th St
Philadelphia
PA 19103
USA
paonedesign@aol.com

Pfadfinderei
91 Oranienburger Str
Berlin 10178
Germany
flori@pfadfinderei.com

Pitch Interactive, Inc.
Suite 208, 812 East Dayton
Madison
WI 53703
USA
wes@pitchinteractive.com

Plazm
P.O. Box 2863
Portland
OR 97208
USA
seg@plazm.com

Emmanuel Prado
5561 Buchardo
Buenos Aires 1765
Argentina
emmanuelprado@gmail.com

Principle
65 Aberdeen St
Quebec
Quebec G1R 2C6
Canada
pamela@designbyprinciple.com

Raidy Printing Group
P.O. Box 175 165
Beirut 2071 3203
Lebanon
design@raidy.com

Reich + Petch
1867 Yonge St
Toronto
Ontario M4S 1Y5
Canada
li@reich-petch.com

Richard Sarson Art & Design
53b Barrett's Grove
London N16 8AP
UK
info@richardsarson.com

Julian Rodriguez
Apt. 5°A, 1773 Paroissien
Buenos Aires 1429
Argentina
julianrodriguez@fibertel.com.ar

Stefan Sagmeister
15a, 222 West 14th St
New York
NY 10011
USA
info@sagmeister.com

Simon Winter Design
7 Bedford St
Brighton BN2 1AN
East Sussex
UK
hello@simonwinterdesign.co.uk

The Small Stakes
3878 Whittle Ave
Oakland
CA 94602
USA
jason@thesmallstakes.com

Andy Smith
34 St Helens Park Rd
Hastings TN34 2DP
East Sussex
UK
andy@asmithillustration.com

Staple Design
84 Orchard St
New York
NY 10002
USA
jeff@stapledesign.com

SteersMcGillan Design Ltd.
6–8 Cotterell Ct
Monmouth Pl
Bath BA1 2NP
UK
rmcgillan@steersmcgillan.co.uk

Studio8 Design
1 Sans Walk
London EC1R 0LT
UK
info@studio8.co.uk

Studio A N D
2278, 15th St, Space 4
San Francisco
CA 94114
USA
usa@and.ch

Julieta Vaggi
2671 Ohiggins St
Capital Federal
Buenos Aires 1428
Argentina
chulevaggi@hotmail.com

With Relish Ltd.
154 Evering Rd
London N16 7BD
UK
sarah@withrelish.co.uk

Zion Graphics
Bellmansgatan 8
Stockholm 118 20
Sweden
ricky@ziongraphics.com

Index